YOUR
BRAIN'S
NOT
BROKeN

YOUR BRAIN'S NOT BROKeN

Strategies for Navigating Your
Emotions and Life with **ADHD**

TAMARA ROSIER, PhD

Revell
a division of Baker Publishing Group
Grand Rapids, Michigan

Published by Revell
a division of Baker Publishing Group
PO Box 6287, Grand Rapids, MI 49516-6287
www.revellbooks.com

Printed in the United States of America

Library of Congress Cataloging-in-Publication Data
Names: Rosier, Tamara, 1968– author.
Title: Your brain's not broken : strategies for navigating your emotions and life with
    ADHD / Tamara Rosier, PhD.
Description: Grand Rapids, Michigan : Revell, a division of Baker Publishing
    Group, [2021]
Identifiers: LCCN 2021006605 | ISBN 9780800739423 (paperback) | ISBN
    9780800741334 (casebound) | ISBN 9781493431984 (ebook)
Subjects: LCSH: Attention-deficit disorder in adults. | Attention-deficit disorder in
    adolescence. | Attention-deficit hyperactivity disorder.
Classification: LCC RC394.A85 R67 2021 | DDC 616.85/8900835—dc23
LC record available at https://lccn.loc.gov/2021006605

The names and details of the people and situations described in this book have been changed or presented in composite form in order to ensure the privacy of those with whom the author has worked.

In keeping with biblical principles of creation stewardship, Baker Publishing Group advocates the responsible use of our natural resources. As a member of the Green Press Initiative, our company uses recycled paper when possible. The text paper of this book is composed in part of post-consumer waste.

23   24   25   26   27   7   6   5

To the ADHD posse—Brooke, Kaitlynn, Megan, and Tom.
Thank you for your daily inspiration. We're all in this together.

To the neurotypicals—Lauren, Adam, and Ridge.
Thank you for your love, your patience, and
lending us your prefrontal cortices every once in a while.

CONTENTS

Contents

ACKNOWLEDGMENTS

While writing this book, I slipped into all of the malicious motivational snares that I write about in chapter 6—avoidance, anxiety, procrastination, anger, shame, and self-loathing. I want to thank my family and others who helped me confront those manipulative scoundrels.

To my husband, Tom Emigh: You believe that "properly supported," I can do anything. You are my proper support. Thank you so much for listening as I worked out my ideas.

To my children with ADHD, Kaitlynn Tefft, Brooke Rosier, and Megan Lorenz: Thank you for all that you have taught me about your experiences with ADHD. It has been a privilege to walk beside you as you matured. I am so relieved that you all grew up to be the beautiful adults you are. You kept me guessing for a little bit.

To my child who doesn't have ADHD and kept asking if she could be in this book, Lauren Rosier: Here you are. I study you when I want to understand how a neurotypical thinks. Thank you for your consistency, love, and patience with those of us who are consistently inconsistent.

To my son-in-law, Adam Lorenz: Thank you for your encouragement to write a book proposal and for believing that I had something to say. Your encouraging texts chased away the malicious motivators.

To my writing coach, Lissa Halls Johnson: Thank you for convincing me to abandon my academic-toned voice for something real. Your gentle prodding helped me develop more confidence. You were this book's doula.

To the fantastic team at Revell: Thank you to everyone on the Revell team who helped me so much. Special thanks to Andrea Doering, acquisitions editor, for the opportunity to tell my ADHD stories. Her team of editors, Kristin Kornoelje and Jessica English, polished the text. I appreciate your attention to detail. Thank you to Laura Palma for the cover design.

To Oren and Chris Mason at Attention MD: Over ten years ago, Chris and I met for coffee. "You should be an ADHD coach," she said. And for once, I followed directions. Thank you to both of you for supporting my career in this field from the beginning.

Finally, to my clients: there would be no book at all without you. Each of you gives me a deeper insight into what it is like to have ADHD. Thank you for sharing your journey with me.

INTRODUCTION

No More Pretending

Put me at any large party, networking event, or fundraiser, and I will naturally gravitate toward the individuals in the room with ADHD. This isn't intentional, It just happens. It's not because I founded the ADHD Center of West Michigan, nor because I have worked in this field for over twelve years. It's not because three of my four children have ADHD. It's because I instinctively know my tribe. You see, I also have ADHD. But you most likely wouldn't see it—at first.

The symptoms of ADHD are mostly invisible—unless you know where to look. For the most part, others wouldn't notice that I struggle to sit still, because I don't visibly fidget much, and I don't get up and move around when I shouldn't. Instead, I secretly keep myself busy by wearing jewelry I can fidget with or tracing the ridges of the glass in my hand.

In social situations, you might not see all the ways I am trying to fit in, nor that it takes a tremendous amount of energy to look "normal." I am continuously working diligently to suppress ADHD tendencies by pretending that I care about polite small talk, not interrupting people, and listening carefully. Eventually, the combination of pretending to be a grown-up and hog-tying impulsive thoughts and actions causes social fatigue. So I wander toward the people who are more like me—the impish and interrupting type. With other people who have ADHD, conversations bounce around many topics in a freestyle stream of consciousness. Now I'm no longer pretending to fit in. I am not overly focused on ADHD symptoms. I am in the moment, enjoying the party and being comfortable with my ADHD self.

Unless you spend time with me, you may not know how ADHD affects me daily. You may see me struggle, however, to remember things, to pay attention in meetings, to listen to directions, to complete tasks. You are very likely to see me look for misplaced items, mumbling to myself, "Now where could that be?" If you don't know that those are symptoms of ADHD, you may judge me as irresponsible, scattered, untrustworthy, or even just dumb. That's because the symptoms of ADHD are often misconstrued and judged as character traits instead of seen as a result of neurological differences.

Because I know that many people don't understand ADHD and misunderstand the symptoms they see, I do my best to look "normal"—which requires me to fake it. Each day I struggle with the apparently simple tasks in life. For example, I would like to call and meet my friends for coffee, but anything that isn't happening *right now* seems too overwhelming to plan. Some days I feel like I can't get my scattered thoughts in order long enough to start a task, let alone stay on track and finish it. Sometimes my attempts to bury my symptoms fail miserably. Little ADHD errors throughout my day pile up: I double-book clients, forget to pay a bill, or leave my car windows open on a rainy day. By evening, I am exhausted and feel like a failure. And I am sure that others see me as a failure too.

I know too well how those of us with ADHD are assessed by a non-ADHD world. Previous supervisors, friends, and even family members have interpreted my symptoms as carelessness, laziness, or stupidity. Even when people know that I have ADHD, they often attribute my symptoms to flaws in my character, telling me to pay more attention to this or that.

I frequently speak to various groups about how ADHD affects individuals. On one such evening, I was talking to a large group of parents on the topic of raising emotionally healthy children who have ADHD. During the session, I highlighted the importance of empowering their children to problem-solve. I explained how easily people with ADHD feel shame and inadequacy. Afterward, some of the parents formed a line to ask additional questions, and I helped the participants develop the next steps in their parenting. A well-meaning non-ADHD parent came up to me at the podium and said, "I will take your glass. I know you will forget to do it," then winked and laughed at her own joke. I must have looked shocked, because she stopped and said, "Oh, did you need this glass?"

Her words had felt like a slap to my face. She had assumed I would forget and made a punch line out of my struggles, landing the all-too-familiar jab, "I will do this for you because you are too careless/stupid/unreliable to do it." I had already made allowances for my forgetfulness by placing the remote control I was using next to the glass so I wouldn't leave it behind.

On the flight home, I reflected on how easily I could feel inept. I wished the woman had just said, "I would love to take care of this for you." I know she really didn't mean to send the negative message that I was careless. But because those of us with ADHD receive so many small messages like that, they build up and leave dents in our sense of well-being.

Part of this problem is how others judge me, but another part is how hard I judge myself. Like so many with ADHD, I am sensitive to rejection and criticism. I make the cognitive mistake of seeing criticism where it wasn't intended, such as with that helpful parent at the conference.

I have tried to hide my natural way of thinking or behaving from people so that I can fit into a non-ADHD world. I have studied the patterns of non-ADHD people—how they think and act—to help me blend in. I have come to the conclusion that I cannot fake being neurotypical any longer. Instead, I need to be honest about how ADHD affects me, how I think, and how I tend to act, then use that understanding to help me navigate the world in which I live. It is a constant game of accommodating, but it works! I don't need to pretend any longer. I accept that I am different from others who don't have ADHD. And even though I live in a fast-paced, detailed world full of distractions, I can figure out how to navigate by continually developing new skills and attitudes. Learning how my brain tends to function helps me develop hacks and workarounds to get things done and to be gracious to myself when I don't.

If you have ADHD, you need to know that your brain is not broken. It doesn't work in the same way as a "normal," or neurotypical, brain does because it's wired differently. Some parts of the ADHD brain are overactive compared to the non-ADHD brain, and some are underactive. Seeing how the ADHD brain works differently from the neurotypical brain helps us understand, accept, and compensate for our differences.

This knowledge that ADHD is a complicated disorder that affects each part of a person's life is the first step to managing it. It is my desire for you to learn to see your ADHD patterns and then make the adaptations necessary for you to live effectively. The knowledge you will gain about ADHD will empower you so that you can manage your symptoms without needing to pretend to others and yourself.

In chapters 1, 2, and 3, you will learn about the complicated emotional landscape of those with ADHD. You will see that emotional difficulty can show up in many different ways. For example, some might have trouble putting the brakes on their feelings when they're angry or stressed about something. Others might struggle to get revved up to do something when they're feeling bored. Spotting the emotional components of ADHD helps to compensate for the impact of it.

Chapters 4, 5, and 6 delve into the ADHD thought life. Persistent negative messages that we send ourselves are common distractors in the ADHD brain. Like naughty little elves, they sneak around, whispering lies that we believe. They implant messages of fear, failure, and unworthiness. You will learn how to identify these cognitive errors, address them, and move on from them.

In chapters 7, 8, and 9, you will learn how people with ADHD understand time, energy, and motivation and how to work within that understanding. You will learn how to use the Solve-It Grid to analyze your tasks and manage your calendar—and, most importantly, to begin to approach life's details in an ADHD-friendly manner.

Chapter 10 presents a way to understand how managing your emotions, thought patterns, and actions contributes to your overall level of emotional health. As the ADHD Ladder of Emotional Health helps you see what is happening in your emotional landscape, you will be able to better manage your moment-by-moment situation and make informed choices.

Chapter 11 brings up the important topic of boundaries. Personal boundaries are guidelines, rules, or limits that a person creates to identify reasonable and safe ways for other people to behave toward them. Many people with ADHD have unhealthy boundaries, which leads to difficulties in managing healthy relationships, balancing activities and rest, and coordinating appropriate emotions to match the situation. Setting boundaries can help you navigate your world more safely and efficiently.

Chapter 12 looks at three practical areas to help you improve your ADHD symptoms—managing your sleep, protecting your peak times, and learning to rehearse tasks. Focusing on these areas will provide you with a solid foundation for creating other ADHD-friendly strategies for your life.

Chapter 13 discusses how to raise emotionally healthy children who have ADHD. You can teach your child the power of self-efficacy and resiliency. Children with ADHD can grow up to be confident adults if given the necessary nurturing and skills.

As the book concludes, you will have learned patience and kindness for yourself as well as for the person you now recognize as having this disorder. Most of all, you will have confidence that although living well with ADHD has its challenges, it is possible to live productively and contentedly.

And Then *Ping!* Goes My Brain

"My brain keeps pinging!" Kristine said, explaining the chaos that ruled her days. "*Ping!* Oh, I gotta remember that. *Ping!* I need to do that now before I forget. *Ping!* Do this. *Ping! Ping! Ping!* All day. Like a berserk iPhone ringing in my head." She let out a long, heavy sigh that turned to tears. "I can't handle it all. I just can't." I handed her the box of tissues on the table as she continued, "Everything's a mess: my car, my apartment. I keep making stupid little mistakes. I'm tired and overwhelmed all the time. I keep telling myself, 'Kristine, you can do better. Get it together!' But it seems like I just can't. My fiancé asks how he can help me—I don't even know what help to ask for. I have so many people willing to help. But what do I tell them to do?"

As she talked, I could hear the frustration spilling out in her words and tone of voice that are typical in adults who share her disorder. Her complaints were far from unusual. Many of my clients, adults of any age or gender, tell variations of the same story. They are exhausted from having so many thoughts that seem to collide at the same time. They are frustrated and angry with themselves for struggling to complete tasks, even ones that seem simple. Yet many explain that they have a strange ability to hyperfocus for hours on some tasks they find interesting. And, like Kristine, they often tell me that they have a tendency to overlook details, leading to errors or incomplete work.

Kristine has a neurological disorder that affects nearly 5 percent of the United States adult population. It's called attention deficit hyperactivity disorder, or ADHD. Adults with ADHD, previously known as ADD, often struggle to regulate attention and impulses due to differences in the way their brains have developed and function. Although ADHD is still often thought of as the naughty-boy disease that will eventually go away with maturity, science now shows that one does not outgrow ADHD. Some symptoms can lessen or disappear as a person gets older, but that is not the same as outgrowing them.

Not only does adult ADHD exist, but it also has an immense impact on the quality of one's life experiences. Most people with ADHD will continue to have symptoms throughout adolescence and adulthood. These symptoms often shift as a person becomes more sophisticated in their approach to life, but the basic ADHD patterns are still present. Some people don't become better at managing their symptoms; they become better at hiding them—until they can't.

I was able to reassure Kristine that she was exhibiting the most common ADHD symptoms among adults: problems with working memory, trouble directing focus, struggles with organization and time management, and emotional hypersensitivity. Like many adults with ADHD, Kristine had been able to compensate for her symptoms when she was younger, but as a young professional amid significant transitions in her life and increasing responsibilities, she felt the strain on her ability to cope. She had just finished graduate school, moved back to her hometown, and started a new job, and she was getting married in a month.

Her difficulty dealing with everyday life is not unusual. The more someone with ADHD tries to manage the complexities of life—pursuing a career, raising a family, running a household—the greater the demand on their abilities to organize, focus, and remain calm. Though these things can be challenging for anyone, for someone with ADHD, it can feel downright impossible.

"People don't have any idea how hard I have to work to do normal stuff," Kristine said, tearing up again. "It's just so hard."

As I listened, I heard the all-too-familiar refrain: *It's hard to be me.* This refrain is not an exaggeration or symptoms of a pity party. When a person has ADHD, it not only *feels* very difficult to manage even the average day-to-day challenges of life; it actually *is* more difficult.

"I feel like that too," I assured her. "Many of us with ADHD do."

I am open with my clients about my own struggles. I want them to know I more than empathize with them and the challenges they face with ADHD; I live it as well.

"Here's what it feels like for me," I told her. "It's like I'm at a starting line of a race. The whistle blows, the pistol fires. As I move, I stumble and fall. Confused, I look down to see why and find that I'm missing a part of my leg! It's clear I won't be able to run like the others, but no one seems to notice my missing appendage. Instead, they expect me to participate in the race like everyone else! They only fault me for the falls I take and my lack of speed and agility."

Kristine's expression changed from sad to intrigued. She was athletic and loved playing sports, so the metaphor made sense to her. "I guess for me it feels like I'm trying to run an obstacle course," she said. "I have stairs to run, tires to dance through, and ropes to climb—and no one gets that half of my leg is missing!" She continued with the metaphor that was now hers. "I tell myself, 'Run faster, Kristine.' But I keep falling. People ask me why I don't run the course like everyone else, demanding I compete with people who have two legs. I know I can't keep up. But what I'm really

21

wondering is, what if I just can't compete in an obstacle course at all?" She paused at the significance of her own question, landing on the distinct disadvantage those of us with ADHD often feel compared to our non-ADHD peers. Our symptoms whittle away at our efficiency in life and erode our beliefs in our own ability to succeed.

I told her that it seemed clear to me that she was working hard at all the things she was doing and then said, "But your challenges aren't about strength or willpower, are they?"

Kristine, like so many of my clients, was frustrated with herself and blamed her failures on a lack of effort or weak character, when the reality was that so many of her struggles were because of a brain that worked very differently than the neurotypical, or non-ADHD, brain.

ADHD's wide variety of frustrating symptoms can hinder everything from relationships to careers. It is invisible and yet unmissable. Once you know what to look for, spotting an ADHD pattern in someone you know becomes clear and obvious. Roberta, a spouse of someone with ADHD, returned from her husband's family reunion and said, "I can see the ADHD patterns of thinking throughout his whole family—but they can't!" She and her husband have been learning how ADHD affects their marriage, and that knowledge has been beneficial in helping them thrive. "Seeing those patterns has helped me develop patience not just for my husband but for that side of the family."

Trouble Directing and Sustaining Attention

There is a misconception that those with ADHD lack the ability to pay attention or stay focused. The reality is that ADHD causes us to pay too *much* attention to everything most of the time—especially when it comes from our environment. We may become easily distracted by irrelevant information that our five senses are detecting: people whispering, crooked artwork on the wall, perfume that is too strong, the itchy tag of our T-shirt, lights that are too bright. Because we don't have the filters to sift out unnecessary information, these distractions, which are nearly invisible to the neurotypical person, compete for our attention. Because of our brains that go *ping!* our attention is often inefficiently redirected.

Bouncing from one activity to another isn't uncommon in individuals with ADHD. Kristine explained how she would flit from one thought or activity to another, and then another and another. Quickly moving between activities leads to a tendency to overlook details, causing errors or incomplete work.

ADHD can help someone focus, however, on tasks they find stimulating or engaging because a specific part of their brain is emotionally invested in the activity. I have a student client, for example, who spends hours reading about World War II. He has dug into original texts examining the thinking of that time. His parents shake their heads because their eighth grader who can process this part of history so deeply didn't pass social studies. World War II is fascinating to this young man, but his routine middle school curriculum isn't.

Because of how the ADHD brain operates, we have a hard time paying attention if something isn't inherently interesting or emotionally engaging. Functions that we find monotonous or mundane create more difficulties for us. That is why we will so often get distracted by lower-priority tasks—they are more interesting or more easily accomplished than our higher-priority tasks.

There is also the "Wait, what?" phenomenon that happens when those of us with ADHD forget to listen. We think we are listening, and then our minds begin to drift. We zone out without realizing it, which leads to difficulty in remembering conversations or following a complex set of directions. This occurs not because we don't care about what is being said but because we have difficulty sustaining our attention for very long.

Hyperfocus

Conversely, sometimes it will look like those of us with ADHD can actually sustain focus, but it's not a normal type of focus. When we deeply and intensely concentrate on something that we find very interesting, we will unconsciously tune out any irrelevant thoughts and senses. This is a single-minded trancelike state called hyperfocus. It's our way of tuning out the chaos inside and outside of our heads. Hyperfocus happens when we completely immerse ourselves in an intriguing task, like working out complicated math problems or editing photos and film. Some of us become so engrossed in a project that it looks like we are completely unaware of anything else happening around us.

A person who is hyperfocused often wears an intense stare, has no perception of time passing, and has no recognition of physical needs (thirst, hunger, etc.). Parents and spouses are often confused by the fact that their loved one can focus on something like a video game, an intricate puzzle, a Lego set, or model building for hours but won't put the same effort into other tasks. This hyperfocus is often interpreted as selfishness, laziness, or defiance.

Hyperactivity or Restlessness

Some people fit the stereotypical ADHD personality, which means they are living out their hyperactivity externally. They talk excessively, attempt to do many things at once, and have trouble sitting still, constantly fidgeting. They are highly energetic and perpetually on the go as if driven by a motor.

However, ADHD expert William Dodson explains that "the vast majority of adults with ADHD are not overtly hyperactive, though they are hyperactive internally."[1] For many of them, their hyperactivity feels more like an inner restlessness or agitation. They will likely worry about what may happen in the future. Like their outwardly hyperactive counterparts, they also have racing thoughts and a craving for excitement, but it occurs inwardly.

Impulsivity

Impulsivity is a spin-off of hyperactivity and restlessness combined. That internal churning can cause people with ADHD to have difficulty managing their behaviors, comments, and responses. They might act before thinking or react without considering potential consequences. When they have impulse problems, staying patient is challenging. For better or for worse, they often dive headlong into situations and find themselves in potentially precarious circumstances.

There's the dad who wants to get that play structure erected for his kids, and he rushes through the building process without planning or reading directions and finds he has to go back and rebuild much of it. There's the man who has trouble behaving in socially appropriate ways and frequently interrupts his friends, talking over them in his rush not to forget what he was going to say. There's the employee who has difficulty sitting still in a company meeting, or the person who blurts out thoughts that are rude or inappropriate. Even the repetitive questions from a spouse that can be perceived as nagging can be traced back to ADHD impulsivity. Poor self-control is an issue for some and can lead to acting recklessly or spontaneously without regard for consequences or can contribute to addictive tendencies.

Difficulty Managing Emotions

Although we may not like to talk about it or admit it, many of us with ADHD have a hard time managing our feelings. And because we don't talk about it, people don't understand this emotional side of ADHD. They are unaware that we are very sensitive, experiencing emotions with great intensity.

This emotional hypersensitivity takes on a variety of forms. First and most importantly, what would be a small emotional event to most people would feel like a big event to those of us with ADHD. When our ADHD brains confuse what is a big deal and what is a small deal, we can respond to minor irritations with the same intense emotional energy as we would in dangerous situations. Fueled by our exaggerated emotions, we overreact to criticism with fear of rejection, worries that we are inadequate, low self-esteem, and insecurity. Something as simple as a forgotten library book can bring deep shame and embarrassment. A store clerk's flippant comment about our messy purse is crushing and puts us into hiding for the rest of the day. We may never feel truly confident at work—living in constant fear that we will be fired for any small failure.

We can be more easily flustered, stressed, or irritable. Some of us are short-tempered, exploding in the face of frustrations. Out of frustration over a broken garbage disposal, we snap at our spouse. Or we lash out at a friend because they accidentally spilled water on our paperwork.

When the intensity of our feelings doesn't match the situation, we might realize it and feel embarrassed. Other times we may not even catch that we have overreacted because we see our emotional intensity as normal. Many family members of those with ADHD tell me that they feel like they are walking on eggshells around their spouse or children, working hard not to set them off.

Should I Seek a Diagnosis?

Life can be a balancing act for any adult. But when you have ADHD and don't know it, it's easy to conclude that there's something wrong with you—especially if you don't have a framework for understanding what you are experiencing. Undiagnosed and un-treated ADHD can have wide-reaching effects and cause problems in virtually every area of your life, including home, career, and relationships. These effects can lead to embarrassment, frustration, hopelessness, disappointment, and loss of confidence.

If you recognized yourself in the above descriptions and scenarios, chances are you may have adult ADHD and have suffered over the years in shame and frustration due to this unidentified issue. You may feel like you've been struggling to keep your head above water, overwhelmed by constant stress. Each day your symptoms of trouble directing attention, impulsivity, or difficulty managing your emotions frustrate you to no end. You may even feel like others have labeled you lazy, irresponsible, or stupid because of your forgetfulness or difficulty completing specific tasks, and you may have begun to think of yourself in these negative terms as well. You may feel like you'll never be able to get your life under control or fulfill your potential. For you, a diagnosis of adult ADHD can be an enormous source of relief and hope.

A diagnosis can also often help explain past struggles. After being diagnosed at age forty-five, John exclaimed, "Finally, it all makes sense! I always felt like I was losing my mind. Now I see why some things are just hard for me." Tracking his ADHD patterns helped him strategize and approach things differently. "I now know that I need to take ADHD into account for everything I do." It doesn't change that he has to work harder to achieve the same level of success as his non-ADHD peers, but it helps him understand his ADHD and decide what to do about it.

What about Medication?

Many people with ADHD cannot effectively regulate certain brain chemicals—dopamine, norepinephrine, and serotonin. Medication for ADHD works on brain chemistry to help govern its dynamics. Although medication may not be the solution for everyone, we have pretty good evidence that it works well for a majority of people. Taking medication can help individuals modulate emotions, initiate tasks more quickly, and appear less distracted.

For some people, medication helps their symptoms immensely. Others might improve substantially, and for a few others, medication helps a little but not that much.

However, it is not advisable to rely solely on medication. There's a saying in the ADHD coaching world: "Pills don't teach skills." This truth reminds those of us with ADHD that we still need to develop specific skills and strategies for managing the details of a modern, complex world. Learning how ADHD affects our lives daily will help us develop healthier behavior patterns.

Yes, Having ADHD Is Difficult, But . . .

For those of you who are neurotypicals, my hope is that after reading this book, when you come across a person who appears disorganized or manic or just can't seem to get it together, you will reach for your compassionate understanding and become a part of the solution rather than adding to that person's guilt and shame, encouraging them as they run their difficult race.

For those of you who have ADHD, I hope that by the end of this book you will rejoice in the good news that no matter how overwhelming they feel, the challenges of ADHD can be addressed. No matter your age (my oldest client is sixty-five), it's never too late to begin tackling the symptoms. With knowledge about ADHD, support of loved ones, effective strategies, and possibly medication, you can learn to manage your "pinging" brain and start feeling good about your life again.

2

Elves, Dirty Babies, and Lucille Ball

"Why is this so hard?" Claire asks as she forces herself out of bed in the morning. Getting up, completing essential hygiene routines, tending to the dogs, and then getting them all out the door on time with the day's necessities in hand feels unreasonably difficult. She has no doubt that the process should be easier and more natural than it is.

Like many people with ADHD, Claire usually finds waking up in the morning to be unpleasant, so she delays the inevitable discomfort of starting her day, hitting the snooze on her alarm and pulling the covers up to her chin. In the office, she jokes with me, "Each morning I go through the five steps of waking up: denial, anger, bargaining, depression, and then finally acceptance." I laugh. The allusion to the grief-cycle emotions is remarkably accurate for her waking experience. Because of sleep cycles and sleep-hygiene habits, many with ADHD find the transition from sleep to wakefulness difficult.

Once she drags herself out of bed, brushing and flossing her teeth feel tedious, and she wonders whether it's necessary to floss. Nemo, her older German shepherd, is reminding her to feed him soon, nudging and directing her to where the food is kept. He knows that after that he is going to doggie day care, so he rounds up his doggie sibling and they sit by the door, waiting. "He doesn't seem to have ADHD," Claire says, amusing us both with her own running commentary.

With her military husband deployed, Claire, a young professional, is left to run the house. In his absence, she finds the basic functions of life overwhelming and exhausting. She wants to be good at life—and she's annoyed that she's not. Although her too-intelligent-for-their-own-good German shepherds demand her physical and emotional attention, she can't use them as an excuse. With or without them, the details of life are overwhelming.

It's not because Claire's not smart enough. She's a lawyer with an undergraduate degree in engineering and two master's degrees—one in engineering and the other in law. She can wrap her mind around extraordinarily complex, technical aspects of her working life, but in her personal life it's the little yet essential functions that seem to stump her.

It's also not because she doesn't want to excel in the basics of her life. She does. She has a driven and ambitious personality. She is the first to arrive at the office and the last to leave. As a natural-born organizer, she is a list maker who finishes everything on those lists—a practical person who can be counted on to get the big things done.

It's not because Claire is lazy either. She is typically an industrious, reliable, honest, and dutiful person. She even developed a personal value system where she determined what is meaningful and important to her. This set of principles and ideals provides her with structure and purpose, guiding her choices and behavior.

If Claire's struggles are not because of her intellectual capacity, her personality, or her character, then what is the problem? She is terrible at the easy things in life because she has ADHD—and she is tired of them all. Her ADHD brain sabotages her in so many ways, but the thing she hates the most is the distortion of her perception of time. This distortion causes an inability to accurately assess the amount of time an activity takes. Predicting how long it will take to blow-dry her hair, drive downtown to her law firm, run errands, and get from point A to point B is more difficult for her than being a lawyer. These issues make her everyday experiences more difficult for her than for her non-ADHD peers.

Claire joins the multitude of individuals with ADHD who find simple tasks difficult. She is not the only one to wonder, *Am I really that dumb?*

Many coaches and counselors assume that to begin solving these problems, they need to address each of Claire's symptoms and fix them. I have found that it is more effective to take a different approach. I begin by asking clients to create a metaphor—a word picture—of how they see their ADHD. Although there are themes and patterns to behavior, ADHD can present very differently from person to person, and metaphors help me understand those differences. Some folks describe the destructive nature ADHD has on their lives as an uncontrollable tornado that whips through anything they try to accomplish, or as a monster lurking in the shadows. Once I understand how my clients are seeing their ADHD, we can begin to discuss ways to resolve the metaphor. Taking a holistic approach like this helps clients see the big picture, identify what can be changed, and learn to problem-solve in real time.

For example, before Claire could address her frustrations with her daily life, she needed to understand how she has viewed her ADHD. The first time I asked Claire to create a metaphor of her ADHD experience, she couldn't. After a few sessions, she found a way to describe it: "I imagine my ADHD as a mischievous little elf that creeps in and moves things. He plays with time using a remote that can control the speed of time: fast-forward or slow motion." Now that she could create a word picture of her symptoms, she could identify how she wanted to address them. Claire wanted to talk about her elf problem, so she created strategies to outwit her ADHD elf.

The Dirty Baby and Other Mental Pictures

"You want to know how I see my ADHD?" Melanie said. "It's a dirty baby."

Melanie was in her forties and was recently diagnosed with ADHD. Her husband and four boys all had it, and before the diagnosis, she thought that she was the neurotypical one, the glue that held her family together. She was good at managing schedules, keeping the house tidy, and organizing daily life for a full house. By all accounts she looked like she had it all together: a loving wife and mother in a well-run home.

She credited her four years in the army with teaching her good organizational skills. "There's one way to do things in the army, and you do it that way," she explained. "It just made my life easier." When she took a job as a scrub nurse in a local hospital, her structural, organizational skills were cemented. She followed protocols to do what needed to be done. Yet she felt like she struggled as a nurse: "I always felt different from the other nurses. Doing the smaller, easier parts of the job came so quickly to them. I worried about those details much more than the big things. As a result, I never felt like a good nurse." But in fact, she was considered by her peers to be an outstanding nurse and was recognized for her quick thinking on more than one occasion.

Now a stay-at-home mom, Melanie spends her summer days protecting the refrigerator and pantry from being ransacked by marauding bands of growing boys—her sons and their friends. Since being diagnosed, Melanie said, "My life is starting to make sense now." That part of herself that she couldn't entirely trust, the dirty baby, was ADHD. "No matter how many times I wash him, he's always messy." I giggled at her metaphor and then stopped at her serious look. "I really hate how the dirty baby makes me feel overwhelmed and angry. Some days, I just end up hating myself." Melanie was beginning to understand how menacing the emotional dysregulation associated with ADHD feels.

Others share how their ADHD makes them feel unqualified for basic tasks. Kelly explained that she felt like Lucille Ball. "As a kid, whenever I was stuck at home with a cold, I loved to cuddle on the couch with my mom and watch reruns of *I Love Lucy*." Her childhood memory of watching the goofy antics of Lucy fed her metaphor for her ADHD. "Remember the one where Lucy and Ethel work at the chocolate factory?"

I laughed—it's my favorite too. In that episode, the women stop at the Acme Employment Agency, and Mr. Snodgrass places them as candy makers at Kramer's Kandy Kitchen. The fiasco begins when Lucy is assigned to the candy-dipping section, where she gets into a chocolate-slinging fight with a coworker. Ethel doesn't do well in the boxing room either. The best friends end up assigned to the wrapping assembly line, where their task is to wrap every chocolate candy as it goes by on a conveyor belt. The conveyor belt speeds up, forcing Lucy and Ethel to eat the sweets and stuff them in their hats and blouses.

"That's me!" Kelly explained. "Either I'm hurling chocolate at someone, or the conveyor belt in my life is coming so fast that I'm stuffing chocolates down my shirt."

After we discussed the Lucy debacle, it was easier to develop strategies with Kelly, as I understood what she needed the most. She wanted techniques for managing what seemed to be an endless parade of daily tasks that soon came at her so fast that they felt overwhelming, and she wanted help in managing her emotions so that she didn't get into "chocolate fights."

Another client, Rick, talked about his frustration with himself. He told me he thought of his ADHD as a test that he didn't study for. "I hate that I don't feel prepared for anything, even when I try to plan. As a result, I let people down." The constant feeling that he couldn't keep up led him to feel that he was living behind a mask. "I'm ashamed of who I am, so I try to show the world a different version of me by hiding the parts of myself that I find embarrassing. So I wear a mask that shows an organized, calm, and confident me."

My own ADHD metaphor comes from my favorite field-day activity as a child—the three-legged race. My best friend, Mindy, and I practiced during our spring recesses for the event. We used our belts to strap our legs together, draped one arm over the other's shoulders, and began. "One AND two AND one AND two," we chanted as we worked together. Our efforts paid off. In third grade, we won first place and received a blue ribbon.

These days, instead of fastening my leg to Mindy's, I feel like it is tied to the ADHD version of me. Each morning I get up and give her a little pep talk about that day's race to remind her how we need to work together. "We can do this. One AND two AND one AND two . . ."

The ADHD version of me never fails to let me down. Halfway through the race, she sees a dandelion and sits down to explore it. I try to keep moving, clumsily dragging her a short way. "I'm going to check if you like butter," she says and rubs the dandelion under my chin. "Oh, it's yellow! You like butter!" She laughs. I frown, unamused. Not only am I irritated at her distraction, but she is hindering me from running the race. I try to drag her farther, but I can't. Frustrated, I sit down too. I'm tired from the extra work of hauling her around. I know that if I could just run without her, I would do well.

Metaphors Are Important

Metaphors (and their cousin, similes) go beyond just comprehension and demonstration—they actually change the way we think of a concept on an unconscious level. In a study about how metaphors affect our thinking, half of the participants read about a crime-ridden city where the criminal element was described as a beast preying upon innocent citizens (an animal metaphor). The other group read nearly the same description of the city, but it described the criminal element as a disease that plagued the town (a disease metaphor).

Later, when asked how to solve the crime issue, those who read the animal metaphor suggested control strategies—increasing police presence, imposing stricter penalties. Those who read the disease metaphor suggested diagnostic or treatment strategies—seeking out the primary cause of the crime wave, bolstering the economy. If it was a beast, it needed to be controlled. If it was a disease, it needed to be treated. This study shows that changing the metaphor changed the way readers thought about the issue.

The metaphor we use to describe our ADHD can help us unlock how we address it. It helps us name the parts of it.

How about you? How would you describe your ADHD? What is your metaphor? Take a moment to reflect on how you view this part of yourself, and create a word picture of it. It doesn't matter what your word picture is. You can use whatever metaphor works for you to get a better idea of how you view your ADHD and to change your perceptions of it strategically. Claire looked out for distracting elves. Melanie decided to take care of her dirty baby. Kelly developed skills for managing the chocolates on the conveyor. Rick learned to put down his mask as he practiced a slower pace, allowing him to check in with his true thoughts and feelings before creating plans. And I have learned to have patience when trying to run a three-legged race.

As you read this book, it will be helpful to have your metaphor at the ready. As you name the parts of ADHD, your metaphor will assist you in problem-solving your own frustrations.

Once you have chosen your metaphor, consider what type of reader you are. How you approach the information in this book may help you apply the ideas to yourself or someone you love.

Which Type of Reader Are You?

When I watch a movie on TV, I make sure I am prepared to immerse myself in the experience. I'll get a cozy blanket in the winter and make sure I have enough of my favorite snack and the perfect beverage to go along with it. I've got my remotes and pillows and am ready to press play.

Before you dive into this book, I want you to be prepared to immerse yourself in the experience. Now that you are learning about your ADHD symptoms and have an image of your ADHD, let's consider two more questions before settling in:

- Why are you reading this book?
- What do you hope to gain from it?

There are usually three types of people who will read a book like this—the wanderer, the puzzler, and the laser focused. The first type of reader, the wanderer, doesn't have a definite goal for reading this book. They are the I-liked-the-cover-and-picked-it-up or the my-mom-told-me-to-read-it sort of reader. They don't know what they don't know—yet. It is absolutely okay to be this type. If you are, it may help if you ask yourself these questions:

- What might I want to get from reading this book?
- What is my essential interest in ADHD?
- What do I want to know about how ADHD relates to the rest of my life?

The second type of reader, the puzzler, is actively trying to put the pieces of information about ADHD together. They are already asking themselves questions like, "What is ADHD? How does it affect me or my loved ones?" Readers like this realize there is much more to ADHD than they first imagined. Sometimes they may feel overwhelmed by what seems like too much information to grasp and master. If you are this type of reader, you will be learning many new things, but you don't need to know them all at once. The questions in this book are designed to help you process your thoughts as you move through the chapters. Take your time with each of the ideas in this book.

Haven't found yourself in the first two descriptions? Then maybe you are the third type of reader, the laser focused. You already know a lot about ADHD. You've read other books, you've listened to podcasts, and you either have firsthand experience or have watched someone you love work on managing ADHD. You know there is still more to learn, so you're reading this book. If you are this reader, look for the application questions throughout the chapters. They will help you concentrate on relating the topics to your life.

No matter which type of reader you are, I hope that you will enjoy this book, integrate the stories and advice into your thoughts, and approach ADHD in a more meaningful way.

3

The Case of the Missing Butler

They met in their senior year of college and were immediately attracted to each other. He liked her extroverted, optimistic, and fun-loving personality. She admired his obvious intelligence that presented in a conscientious and ethical way. He had a strong sense of right and wrong. He was well organized, orderly, and meticulous—unlike her parents and her chaotic childhood in so many ways. He did his best to maintain high standards. So when Todd proposed on a chilly May afternoon during a hike on the Lake Michigan sand dunes, Becky said yes.

Becky and Todd married and did the things that young couples do—they established a life for themselves. They worked on their careers, bought a house, and started a family. They made a very nice living in a Midwestern city. He was moving up in the engineering company where he put in full days, and she was a full-time mother with an interior design business on the side. They lived in a lovely house and were active leaders in their church. Their three children were excellent representatives of the lives they'd built—smart, athletic, and witty. From the outside looking in, you might be impressed. They had it all.

But they were in trouble. Todd had a short fuse. Seemingly minor irritants would trigger a screaming fit, leaving Becky feeling unsure of what had just happened. And he seemed worse with unstructured time. Weekends and vacations became a nightmare for Becky as small miscommunications turned into three days of bickering, scolding, or, worse, not speaking at all. Becky recalled one time she questioned why he was taking a particular route home. "I was more curious than anything. I assumed he knew something I didn't." He met her inquiry with accusations of her being controlling and confrontational. That led to a five-day fight in which he refused to speak to her. He didn't speak to her during family meals, during bedtime rituals with the children, or even during the "couple" time set aside at the end of each day for them to just be together.

Sometimes he had quick rebounds. There were times when Becky, still licking her wounds from his harsh words spoken before breakfast, would get a cheery phone call at noon from Todd wondering how her day was going. "It was as if nothing had been said," she recalled. "As if it had never happened."

Becky, confused and becoming bitter, often thought, *This moody, irrational man is not the intelligent, well-organized man I fell in love with.* She was exhausted from the emotionally tumultuous ocean of her marriage. She considered separation—and even divorce—but decided to stay in the relationship. It seemed best for the kids. And she did love him.

Then Becky's life became even more complicated. Her oldest son, Ian, was having difficulties in high school. Up until this time, he had straight A's. Now he was barely keeping up C's. He was temperamental too—in different ways from his father but, like his father, always over minor irritations. Things that her other kids would brush off, Ian would hold on to. If he felt slighted somehow, he would ruminate and stoke his sense of disparity or injustice.

When Becky went looking for answers, a teacher suggested that Ian may have ADHD. Becky couldn't figure out how the teacher had come up with that diagnosis but took her son to a doctor anyway. There she learned the teacher had been correct. Ian's intense feelings, low frustration tolerance, agitation, and quick temper flares were part of the emotional aspect of someone who has ADHD.

The more Becky educated herself about the emotional side of ADHD, the more her experiences with her husband started making sense. Up until now, she had considered ADHD to be a naughty-boy disease caused by poor parenting. She learned that ADHD is a lifelong issue that is not caused by poor parenting but rather by the ADHD brain, which works very differently than a non-ADHD brain. Many of the problems she was seeing with her son—and her husband—fit into the examples of ADHD emotional dysregulation symptoms that she read about. As she researched the disorder, she learned about the disturbing and painful emotional landscape of those with ADHD.

Intense Emotions

Many times, individuals with ADHD feel strong emotions that appear extreme or exaggerated to others. Recent research reveals that those with ADHD can become significantly more frustrated, can lose their tempers more frequently, and are generally more excitable than non-ADHD individuals. The fluctuating and distorted emotional responses contribute extensively to challenges in home life, school, and careers. For the most part, these big emotions are normal in every way except for their intensity.

This difficulty managing emotions can show up in a variety of ways. Some might have trouble putting the brakes on their feelings when they're angry or stressed. Others might use emotions to rev themselves up to accomplish something when they're feeling bored.

41

Those who struggle with emotional regulation tend to

- become quickly frustrated by minor annoyances
- fret too much or too long about small issues
- feel a sense of urgency to get something they want in the moment
- have difficulty calming down after becoming annoyed or angry
- feel deeply wounded or take offense at even the most gentle criticism

When Becky saw this list, she recognized both her son and her husband in it. The list helped her consider that maybe Todd wasn't an angry jerk after all. Even though his actions were painful to others, he may not have understood what was happening to him.

Like a Light Switch

Folks with ADHD are often like a light switch when it comes to their emotions, motivations, and actions. When presented with a task, they will most likely respond with one of two settings or emotional responses: *on* (intense emotion—passionate, fixated, highly motivated) or *off* (little or no emotion—disinterest or little motivation). Becky observed, "Either Todd totally cares about something or he doesn't care at all and doesn't want to do it."

People without ADHD, like Becky, seem to have the benefit of a built-in dimmer switch for their emotions, motivations, and actions. They have more choices and a range of responses. Instead of on or off, they have many gradients of light. Their ability to modulate gives them the advantage of having a "meh" response to a task. When asked to take out the trash, they are likely to think, *I don't really want to do it, but, meh, I will.*

The Hard Work of Remembering

Many individuals with ADHD have an inadequate working memory, which may explain, in part, the light-switch effect. Short-term memory acts as a kind of Post-it Note for temporary recall of information being processed at any point in time. We use the Post-it Note as a place to remember and process information at the same time. Those with ADHD have tiny Post-it Notes with inadequate adhesive. One client quipped, "I use invisible ink on my Post-it Notes." That is to say, it is challenging to hold, access, and use the information in the short-term memory and working memory. As a result, those with ADHD often appear disorganized, short-tempered, or impulsive.

One afternoon, my husband, his brother, and I were watching our kids play skee-ball. We had told the kids that if their combined scores added to a certain amount, we would buy them ice cream. (We often presented silly challenges like this to our children.) My ADHD husband started patting his pockets for his phone, saying, "We're going to need to write this down."

My brother-in-law responded, "You don't need to write it down. I'll just keep track of it in my head."

Both my husband and I looked at him in awe—and then envy. We exchanged looks that said, *I bet he doesn't even appreciate his short-term memory.* Many neurologically typical people don't recognize how easy their life is made by a nicely functioning short-term memory.

Those of us with short-term memory issues feel like we are trying to catch bubbles a child has blown with a plastic wand. They float in front of us, but as soon as we touch them, they pop and are gone. We become frustrated at our lack of ability to hold a minor thought. For example, when my attention is diverted for just a second by my dogs barking at the UPS driver, I shush them, turn around, and think, *What was I just doing?* I try to re-create my most recent thoughts by pushing through the brain fog, attempting to pick up the thought trail I had lost. "Ugh. This is so irritating," I mumble to myself. On a bad day, when I'm tired, hungry, or unmedicated, I stomp around and mutter, tempted to express a slurry of emotions. If it's a good day and I have the ability to exercise self-regulation, I've learned to take a few deep breaths that tell my brain that I am okay, and I begin the act of retracing or re-creating.

Sometimes, because of the working-memory impairment, an intense emotion floods the brain of someone with ADHD. Becky now can recognize it. "When I see Todd grumbling to himself as he's working on his computer, looking and sounding agitated," she says, "I remind myself that he is taxing his short-term memory with some mundane task. He isn't angry, really. He is doing what he can to complete a task."

The Butler and the Angry Neighbor

Challenges with emotions begin in the ADHD brain. To understand them, we first need to know how the brain works in those without ADHD.

The front part of the brain is called the prefrontal cortex (PFC). Tap on your forehead and you are in the general area. This is where executive functioning takes place—those mental processes that include things like planning, short-term memory, working memory, decision-making, and impulse management. In a way, the prefrontal cortex acts like a calm, rational butler, directing behavior and managing emotion.

Those with a normally functioning PFC (those who do not have ADHD) have a great short-term memory. It usually functions predictably and effortlessly. "Sir," the PFC butler calmly states, "you left your keys on the table." Or, "Madam, it is time to leave if you want to stay on schedule." Without the person even being aware of it, their PFC butler is properly managing the details of modern life. Bills get paid on time, plans get made, keys aren't misplaced as often, and time, for the most part, is well managed.

The basic practices of a functioning adult are accomplished with little effort in the PFC.

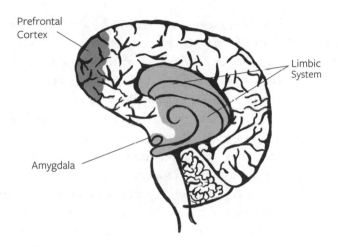

Prefrontal Cortex

Limbic System

Amygdala

The problem arises when individuals with ADHD have limited access to their PFC. Their butler either is silent or has left town altogether. Instead of relying on the PFC butler for planning, short-term memory, and impulse management, those with ADHD rely on the emotional centers in their brain to remember things, make decisions, and motivate themselves. They use emotions to think, react, remember, plan, and act.

Instead of having a tranquil butler in the prefrontal cortex, quietly managing life's small tasks, they have something more like an angry neighbor outside the prefrontal cortex in the emotional centers of their brain, shaming and threatening them. The angry neighbor takes over when the PFC butler is overly challenged by a task that would usually be performed in the front part of the brain. The disheveled old curmudgeon shakes his fist and threatens, "If you lose your keys again . . . !"

Occurrences that don't commonly elicit an emotional reaction become emotional. Individuals with ADHD begin to listen for that angry neighbor who waves his fist, feeling strong negative emotions to "help" them remember their keys. Paying attention to this neighbor does improve their performance a little bit—but not consistently.

When the butler is missing or the Post-its have fluttered away, those with ADHD are filled with a good deal of stress as they try to remember. Because they can't rely on short-term memory in their PFC, they will emotionally mark a memory in a different location of the brain—a place of deep emotions. This is a widespread and mostly unconscious hack that most of them learn in childhood. The mere potential of losing their keys is combined with ugly feelings like anger, anxiety, shame, and self-loathing. The ugly feeling leaves a longer-lasting trail to remembering the location of their keys than their damaged working memory ever could. When they rehearse that negative feeling, they are creating emotional pathways to help them remember their keys in the future. Having to remember in this manner is energy intensive, but sometimes it might be all someone has, especially if they don't take medication. (In chapter 6, we will discuss how those with ADHD have learned to harness those big, negative emotions to motivate themselves.)

The Effect of Big Emotions

"I wish I hadn't punched the wall," twenty-five-year-old Cameron said. He cradled his wrapped hand as he described a recent episode when he lost control of his emotions. "I had no idea I felt so strongly." He stopped, his brow furrowing. "Did I feel strongly? I could make up reasons why I lost it, but did I really feel so strongly that I would go ballistic? What was that?"

Cameron had experienced a hijacking by an intense emotion, an event not uncommon for those with ADHD. Many clients tell me stories about the surprising strength of their emotions that blindside them, blocking their ability to think in a rational way. Because these emotions change at lightning speed, the person doesn't have time to reflect or analyze before speaking or taking action. Instead, they become overwhelmed, fasten onto that intense emotion—in Cameron's case, anger—and crowd out other relevant information that might help them modulate a response. When this happens, they are embarrassed by the strength of their emotions and ashamed of the way they feel and the problems created by their emotional reaction. Many try to hide this emotional intensity—with mixed results.

When I met Todd for the first time, he told me, "I get feedback at work that I can be cold—that I have no feelings. Of course I have them. Inside, I feel deep anger and feel like screaming at someone for screwing up or delaying a process. But I can't let my emotions out as strongly as I feel them. I've done that before and had to apologize to my team. It was humiliating! So I've learned to shove those emotions aside. It's not easy, that's for sure!"

Ignoring the magnitude of feeling is not an adequate solution. One can't simply stuff emotions and expect them to dissipate. Those emotions will find a way to unstuff themselves—usually at an inopportune time.

Todd was a good example of how that works. He clasped his hands and stared at the floor, saying, "When I'm home, it's the opposite. Becky tells me that I have too much emotion."

Becky nodded. "I could understand if he's upset at big things. But Todd flies off the handle over minor issues."

He slowly shook his head. "I'm not sure what to do. Should I just stuff everything like I do at work?" He looked up at me. "Am I really that awful to live with?" He looked at his shoes again. I could tell he was scared. He was bothered by more than how he treated his wife and family. He had great fear that he had a fatal character flaw that could not be addressed. He was afraid that his big emotions made him a bad person. And he didn't know how to manage them. He didn't see many options and felt broken and hopeless. He would soon learn that his intense emotions are a symptom of ADHD.

When those of us with ADHD are listening through our big emotions, we misinterpret what is being said. We listen for what we think are the meta-messages, the big meaning of what people are saying. In a way, we create stories in our minds that interpret events in a certain way, fortifying a broken belief system. When Becky asked Todd to take out the trash, he found himself immediately being defensive. "She doesn't think I do anything around here! Well, I do!" During a session, Becky shrugged and said, "I really was just asking him to take out the trash."

Anger and frustration aren't the only negative emotions we feel. Living with big emotions, combined with the frustrations, failures, and negative feedback that we typically receive when we have ADHD, sometimes feels like a deep sadness. To me it feels like a heavy backpack that I carry everywhere. Twenty-something Ellen describes her sadness as an overwhelmed-at-how-hard-life-is feeling, and it makes her cry. "I'm not a depressed person at all," she explains. "Sometimes I just feel overwhelmingly sad."

People like Ellen suffer from dysthymia, a mild but long-term sadness. Ellen explains the result of her low energy and low self-esteem that accompany dysthymia: "I feel lethargic and useless."

ADHD and its big emotions often strike at our self-confidence. Sadness turns into shame. This shame becomes the lens through which everything is viewed, creating harsh internal dialogues. Ellen found that the combination of medication and coaching has helped her sort out which lens she should use as she navigates her thought life.

A person with ADHD may seem insensitive or unaware of the emotions of others. Though they have the capacity for deep empathy, they are not aware of the immediate emotional impact they have on those around them. I have received texts from adolescent clients saying something to the effect of, "You need to talk to my mom. She started yelling at me for no reason." Texts such as these are often a sign that the adolescent has no clue how surly she has been for a while. And when the parent eventually explodes, the teenager is baffled, asking, "What's her problem?" These high schoolers' surprise is genuine, and their lack of awareness is real. Their behavior appears completely rational to them. But ask Mom and you will hear a common refrain from her (and others who are close to someone with ADHD): "I am exhausted by the emotions."

Not all with ADHD wear those blinders. Many children will have outbursts, realize later how wrong they were, and make genuine, tearful apologies. "I don't know why I said that," one boy explained to his mother as they processed his meltdown. Grownups, on the other hand, are a bit more stubborn. Some are fearful that if they confess their poor behavior, they are admitting they are unlovable or unworthy. Some believe that if they apologize, their loved one will use it against them.

Managing Big Emotions

Medication is an option for treating emotional dysregulation and gives people with ADHD the same fraction of a second that neurotypical individuals have to feel an emotion coming on and decide whether or not to express it. A nonpharmaceutical approach is for clients to learn how to predict and manage emotional responses to lessen the frequency of unwanted outbursts.

In Todd's case, he was diagnosed with ADHD and began medication. His wife immediately noticed a difference in emotional modulation. But pills don't make skills. Todd had developed unhealthy coping skills over his lifetime that he needed to change. This required that he go through a process of unlearning some patterns and learning new ones to manage his emotional responses.

The first step in managing intense emotions is to learn to see the bigness of them. Imagine placing the intensity of emotions along a continuum from 1 to 10, where 1 equals low or no feeling, almost apathy, and 10 equals intense and strong feeling. Individuals without ADHD will spend most of their day in the center of the spectrum—at 4, 5, or 6—even though they have access to the full continuum.

However, individuals with ADHD find themselves hanging out at one end or the other of this emotional spectrum. They tend to rest at a 1 or 2 with very low emotion, then experience a sudden surge to a 9 or 10, flooding the brain with a single intense emotion. And because those with ADHD get confused between a big deal and small deal, it doesn't take a big issue to swing them to the far end of the continuum. Not even ADHD individuals themselves always understand why these huge emotional swings happen. Many just assume the swings are normal.

For example, I can hop into my closed car in midday during the summer, feel the intense heat and stuffiness, and surge to a 9 on the spectrum. I instantly become irrationally aggravated about my discomfort as beads of sweat gather on my chin, and I am heat crazed and angry at nothing in particular. In my ADHD-friendly family, we refer to this phenomenon of overresponding to intense heat as "heat crazy," or its less intense but still grumbly cousin, "heat cranky." Fortunately, I have worked at becoming aware of my sudden swings and intense emotional reactions to a mundane—and predictable—moment. I open all the windows, turn the air-conditioning on high, and take a deep breath. "No need for a nine," I repeat like a mantra, comforting myself. In cases like this, I have practiced recognizing my intensity and calming it.

When I use the hot car example with my clients, they shrug and say, "Well, it *was* hot." They can understand why I would be so irritated. When I use the example with neurotypical adults, they give me the Labrador-retriever head tilt, as if to say, "What did you expect the car to feel like on a hot summer day?"

Todd had a breakthrough at the end of a session recently. He leaned forward and said, "You mean I feel things more strongly?" I honestly thought he already knew that. But that day it clicked. He used his hand to explain further. "So if this is the normal emotion level, and I feel things here"—he raised his hand well above the normal level, then sat back—"then how much should I be trusting these emotions?"

Making Peace

If you are just seeing your big emotions for the first time and realizing that they can be a problem, be gentle with yourself. Try not to judge your insufficiencies. Instead, work on noticing the intensity and name it with a number if you can. Observe the emotions in slow, steady breaths that tell your body to relax. And by all means, laugh at the situation when you can. "I am angry about the temperature in my car! That's funny. Of all the things to be angry about."

An English professor grading a journal that I had kept for the semester wrote in his comments, "May God's special providence watch over those who feel too much."

I was puzzled. At the time, I had no idea I had big emotions, let alone ADHD. "What did he see in my journal that would suggest big emotions?" I wondered out loud to a friend.

She smiled. "You are very energetic with your emotions."

We can experience good intense emotions as well as the less pleasant ones. We seem to experience happiness, gratitude, and contentment more powerfully than our neurotypical peers and loved ones do. We are passionate and strong-willed people. Some of my clients learn to love their intensity and teach their emotions to fly in formation, like planes maneuvering together in a disciplined, synchronized, predetermined manner. After all, there is nothing wrong with people experiencing intense emotions and wild fluctuations unless they are damaging relationships, using poor problem-solving skills, or harming themselves. Some clients don't enjoy their ardent emotions and are more comfortable releasing them in breathing and calming techniques.

As we work on the negative aspects of having big emotions, we heal the wounded parts of our self-worth and self-confidence. By increasing our self-awareness and finding new coping skills, we decrease our old, dysfunctional ways of engaging with life. It's definitely hard work but worth the effort.

Following the Rabbit

In *Alice's Adventures in Wonderland*, Lewis Carroll writes about a young girl named Alice who follows an intriguing white rabbit under a hedge and into a large hole. Carroll tells us that the rabbit hole "went straight on like a tunnel for some way, and then dipped suddenly down, so suddenly that Alice had not a moment to think about stopping herself before she found herself falling down what seemed to be a very deep well."[1]

Many of us with ADHD often feel like Alice. We pop down a hole to follow a thought, and then another almost-related idea appears. One concept transforms into another and then another. Our thoughts move so quickly that we don't think of stopping ourselves. And before long, we find ourselves far away from our initial idea or task.

Today, when people say they "went down the rabbit hole," they are usually referring to getting sucked into spending way too long reading about or researching something on the internet. For those of us with ADHD, though, rabbit holes are a description of our daily thought process as it takes twists and turns, tangents, and digressions.

Most people who have ADHD have a *divergent thinking pattern* that makes falling down rabbit holes a way of life. Divergent, in this case, means tending to develop in different directions, usually at once. Though the technical name is *divergent thinking*, some people might refer to it as *out-of-the-box, nonlinear,* or *creative thinking*. Those with ADHD naturally gravitate toward this type of thinking; their minds generate ideas far beyond rote thinking or expected boundaries.

Monkey, Monkey, Underpants

The key aspect of divergent thinking is having a thought that begins at one point and then propagates in many directions, usually simultaneously. Ben, a fifty-something client, described his divergent thinking as "a whole bunch of rabbits that get out of their pen all at once, and I don't know which one to chase." Trying to chase all those errant rabbits can be energy draining and overwhelming unless a person learns to manage their thinking.

All of my clients can describe times when they fell down the rabbit hole, when one thought led to another and another. Even if they haven't read *Alice's Adventures in Wonderland*, they share Alice's feeling of wandering through the forest, falling down a hole, and landing in unexpected adventures. As a result, their inner monologue can sound a lot like Lorelai, from the comedy-drama series *Gilmore Girls*, as she sits down to write an important letter:

> I thought I'd just sit down and write . . . whatever comes . . . no judgment . . . no inner critic . . . Ooh, was that a bad idea . . . Because my brain is a wild jungle full of scary gibberish . . . I'm writing a letter . . . I can't write a letter . . . Why can't I write a letter? . . . I'm wearing a green dress . . . I wish I was wearing my blue dress . . . My blue dress is at the cleaner's . . . The Germans

wore gray . . . you wore blue . . . *Casablanca, Casablanca* . . . such
a good movie . . . *Casablanca* . . . The White House . . . Bush . . .
Why don't I drive a hybrid car? I should really drive a hybrid car . . .
I should really take my bicycle to work . . . bicycle, unicycle, unitard
. . . hockey puck, rattlesnake, monkey, monkey, underpants.[2]

Finally, in exasperation, Lorelai declares, "It's a big bag of weird
in there."[3]

Anyone with ADHD understands the "monkey, monkey, underpants" type of situation we end up in. And because it affects every
aspect of our lives, we may feel confused, exhausted, and sometimes dumb.

Instead of calling it "a big bag of weird," I want you to know
that if you resonate with Lorelai's monologue, you probably use
divergent thinking more than you use convergent thinking. Every-
body is capable of both types of thinking, depending on the situation. However, it's natural to lean more toward one or the other
when approaching problems and projects. Some people have a
natural preference for divergent thinking. They are the people
who love to come up with new ideas. They are also most helpful
when solving daunting, complex challenges because they are more
likely to articulate ideas that are new and useful. Neither style of
thinking, convergent or divergent, is superior, but knowing the
differences between the two will help you understand yourself and
develop stronger thinking habits.

Those with divergent thinking patterns are naturally intrigued by
how ideas are connected. They create constellations of linked information in their heads. For example, when divergent thinkers learn
something, they intuitively ask, "What can I make with this idea?"
or "How is this idea connected to other ideas?" A newly graduated
divergent thinking nurse explained, "I love the complicated facets of
my job. I love seeing how different aspects of what I learned work
together. In school, we were only taught small, separate pieces of
knowledge. At work, I see all the pieces and how they relate."

Rote learning—memorizing information based on repetition —is not for those with strong preferences for divergent thinking. Divergent thinkers gather information and learn by playing, imagining, inventing, experimenting, and exploring topics and ideas. Those with divergent patterns love to ask, "What if?" or "Why?" Adam, a computer analyst, realized that he was a divergent thinker in college. "I had what my professor called mathematical intuition. When I came across a problem, I used my logical instinct to pull out an answer. If I couldn't, I'd ask a why question. I realize now that I was kind of a nightmare of a student. In my high school calculus class, I kept asking questions like, 'How can the sum of a bunch of partial derivatives somehow measure the way in which a vector field spreads out?'" He shrugged. "I really wanted to know why."

Adam didn't learn through the traditional step-by-step explanation. Instead, he relied on insight that comes from using divergent thinking. Understanding why and how helped him learn the challenging material.

As you may have guessed, many K–12 teachers lean on a traditional style of thinking and therefore find these types of students difficult to teach. They are more like Alice's sister and learn in a concrete, sequential manner.

Alice's Sister

The rest of the world, it seems, is not like the imaginative Alice we encounter in Wonderland. They prefer a different way of thinking called *convergent thinking*. Convergent thinking is a thought pattern that brings together information that focuses on solving a problem, especially one that has a single, correct solution.

Alice's older sister is a good representative of convergent thinking. In *Alice's Adventures in Wonderland*, Carroll begins the story with his main character, Alice, drifting off to sleep while her older sister gives her a history lesson. After Alice awakens from her fantastical dream, she runs off to have tea, leaving her sister to think. Eventually, Alice's sister drifts off to sleep and finds herself in Alice's dream world. Instead of allowing herself to be completely immersed in the fantasy world, she views it in a detached manner, only "half believ[ing] herself in Wonderland." She remains grounded in reality, aware that "she had to but open [her eyes] again and all would change to dull reality," and the strange sounds of the dream world "would change (she knew) to the confused clamor of the busy farmyard."[4] She restricted her thoughts to those that might be correct and realistic, not fanciful or imaginative.

Alice's sister sorts through her experience in Wonderland differently than Alice. She uses her convergent thinking style to analyze, judge, and decide what she is seeing and hearing. Those who use this style tend to evaluate ideas and then make decisions about which ones to discard. Through the convergent sorting process, some ideas will get tossed out because they're too expensive, too time-consuming, too unrealistic, or too far outside the box, or they require too many resources. Put simply, convergent thinking is the process of strategically weeding through those ideas to find the solution.

We all use both divergent and convergent thinking throughout our lives, but we have strong preferences as to which is our default pattern. Studies suggest that we begin our lives as more divergent thinkers. Children have a high divergence capacity that is reduced as they move into adulthood. Typically, as the use of convergent thinking increases, reliance on divergent thinking decreases. The neurological and physiological differences associated with ADHD make it easier to utilize divergent thinking patterns, so those with ADHD tend to rely on that pattern throughout their lives.

The Benefits of a Possibility Brain

Divergent thinkers have possibility brains. Their minds naturally explore and elaborate on ideas, examining what *could* be. This divergent thinking has many notable strengths. Those who rely on this pattern tend to be more curious and creative, and they conceptualize ideas unusually and uniquely.

ADHD minds with divergent thinking patterns often have an insatiable curiosity manifested by the tendency to ask "why" and to seek connections. This curiosity is fueled by the fascination with many aspects of life that those with ADHD have.

One time at a friend's house, Jodi listened to her friend talk about the chickens and ducks she was raising. "I had so many questions," she remembers. Intrigued by the particular breed of the chicken her friend chose, the Sussex chicken, Jodi asked why she wanted to raise that type.

Another guest at the table asked, "Do you like chickens?" His question seemed to convey the meta-question, "Why are you so interested in this?"

Jodi laughed. "Not especially. I'm just extra curious about everything."

My clients continue to amuse and amaze me with their extra-inquisitive natures. Because they are eager to know and understand, they teach themselves things that they find interesting.

Nine-year-old Ava began our session with the fascinating question/factoid, "Did you know that wombat poop is square?"

I nodded because I actually did know that. Then I said, "What I don't know is how it gets to be square."

She knew. Using her hands in a crunching motion, she explained that the wombat intestine's elasticity helps sculpt the feces into cubes. "They don't have round anuses," she finished matter-of-factly.

Ava was curious about animals, so she was always reading about the animal kingdom. She had a voracious appetite for this subject and wanted to learn as much as possible. The curiosity within her divergent thinking was going to be a great asset to her as she continued to develop her scholarly pursuits.

(Note: Because my own inquiring mind wanted to know, I looked up that information later. Not only was she correct about how the feces was formed, but at that time, it was a new scientific discovery.)

Creative, Original, and Elaborative

Many divergent thinkers throughout history are known for their production of ideas that are unique or unusual. Einstein, Galileo, Mozart, and da Vinci all had possibility brains—they saw things, did things, heard things, and created things that no one else had. My favorite example is the artist, inventor, scientist, engineer, and writer Leonardo da Vinci. His notebooks show us his vast interests, experiences, and talents—and point to his divergent thinking habits. As an engineer, da Vinci conceived ideas vastly ahead of his time, conceptually inventing the parachute, the helicopter, an armored fighting vehicle, and the use of concentrated solar power, along with so many other things. As an artist, he developed methods of representing space, three-dimensional objects, and the human figure that changed the world of art.

Thankfully, you don't need to be a da Vinci–level genius to express your divergent thinking. You have the same streak of originality that he did each time you compose, create, design, integrate, rearrange, reconstruct, reorganize, and revise.

However, not all creativity is apparent. Many individuals with ADHD are considered by others to be creative—although they may not feel like they are. Gabe was diagnosed with ADHD in his forties. "I couldn't understand why my professors in college kept calling me a creative," he said. He never considered himself particularly creative. "I don't paint, draw, or make creative things. I'm in science." But his colleagues note how, as a chemist, he often devises new, original ways of doing things or thinking about things. He won an award for his innovation for analyzing soil content. He laughed as he said, "I wasn't trying to innovate. It came naturally It just made sense." Where his colleagues saw and understood a tried-and-true process, Gabe's possibility mind naturally took him exploring down many paths to find a new way of doing something.

Gabe's story shows the divergent thinking strength of elaboration. He is a natural when it comes to enhancing ideas by providing more detail, improving clarity, and understanding the topic. Many individuals with ADHD don't understand that when they appraise, modify, critique, evaluate, judge, and test, they are using their natural divergent thinking patterns.

Fluent, Flexible, and Funny

How many uses can you think of for a clothes hanger? The more answers you are able to generate, the higher you would score on the divergent thinking trait of *fluency*. An individual who has high fluency has the ability to think of many diverse ideas quickly, creating ideas within a specific category. They often create a deeper understanding of a topic when they are experimenting and brainstorming instead of just remembering information. Many times, I see students of all ages get into trouble for having high fluency. These students ask themselves, "What would happen if . . ." and then act on those thoughts.

One eleven-year-old had a possibility brain that led him to conduct many unsupervised experiments that caused damage to property or people. One such experiment involved the fire department being dispatched to his house after he attempted to make a homemade smoke bomb by combining sugar with potassium nitrate in an aluminum foil ball. His savvy mother, however, saw the value of her son's fluency and taught him to run this simple safety test before he experimented: Does my experiment have the capacity to hurt me? Does my experiment have the capacity to hurt others? Does my experiment have the capacity to hurt property? "Sometimes things still get ruined," she admitted, "but it has stopped him from injuring himself and others."

Flexibility, another divergent thinking trait, is the ability to work in diverse categories of ideas rather than within one specific category of fluency. Those with high flexibility are nonlinear thinkers who are able to hold two opposing points of view in their mind at the same time. "My wife gets really frustrated with me," a CEO client explained. "I can argue both sides of an issue very convincingly. Then she'll ask me, 'Which do you believe?' And I say, 'Both!'" This adaptability enables a person to simultaneously think about and develop different concepts as well as switch between them with ease.

And many times, individuals with divergent thinking traits are *funny*. Research suggests that individuals who have strong divergent thinking patterns combine the strengths of fluency, flexibility, originality, and creativity to entertain themselves and others. My clients of all ages, for the most part, are clever, witty, and even hilarious. It is one of the reasons that I love my job—and my family— so much. One of my adult children quips, "We grew up with just enough dysfunction to be funny." The dinner table, for those of us with ADHD, is a place where our family riffs off each other's jokes and repeats comedic bits from past conversations. Though my neurotypical teenage daughter is mostly entertained, she observes that "we are not like normal families." We aren't. The majority of us have ADHD.

Many of my clients use their humor as a coping mechanism. If they can laugh at a situation, it might not be that bad. I look forward to appointments with Taylor, a very funny client of mine. She usually starts her sessions by telling me a story of her embarrassment, social awkwardness, or clumsiness from the previous week. She started one session with her experience at a gynecological exam. "So I went to the lady doctor yesterday . . ." Before long I was wiping away tears of laughter.

Divergent Thinking in the Workplace

People who have predominantly divergent thinking patterns do well to find careers and employers that allow them to express their originality, creativity, fluency, and flexibility. When they do, they find their work very satisfying. As employees, those with divergent thinking patterns often offer fresh, unusual, unique perspectives.

One of my friends is a very talented artist and professor of art education. In the classroom and in her art, her divergent thinking pattern is celebrated and respected. It wasn't until she entered into administrative roles that she felt the tension between convergent and divergent thinking in the workplace. Because of her divergent process, she approached problem solving through what she called an organic method. She usually sensed problems or gaps in information, identified the difficulties, and sought solutions through trial and error or by forming hypotheses. But that wasn't how the rest of her convergent thinking colleagues worked. "My colleagues are so rigid," she complained over lunch. "They think there's only one way to solve problems." Her divergent thinking trait of originality—the ability to look beyond obvious solutions and generate novel ideas and responses—wasn't as appreciated among leadership as it was in the classroom.

Andrew, a physician, was drawn to the emergency department largely because it was where the excitement, interest, and action were. His job gave him the opportunity to use his divergent thinking traits: creativity, elaboration, fluency, and flexibility. He quickly gathered patient stories and medical information, explored many possible solutions, ran tests, and created connections between ideas. "He is an excellent diagnostician," his supervisor told me. Andrew had the capacity to conceptualize the abstract, multifaceted, and intricate ideas his patients presented.

His supervisor told me, "He's brilliant, but . . ." The "but" in this situation said that Andrew was not managing the downsides of his divergent thinking. His supervisors wanted to minimize patient waiting times and to work quickly. They grumbled that he ordered too many tests and was too slow in making decisions about patient care. Andrew was getting stuck in his ability to expand on an idea, embellish it with details, and create an intricate plan—the divergent thinking trait of elaboration. Because he was more interested in careful diagnostics and differentials, Andrew was not completing his charting in a timely fashion. Instead of keeping up with his notes and codes on patients as he went along, he delayed the task until the end of his shift or even the next day. This created a problem for the hospitals. Without Andrew's notes, they couldn't create bills for their services.

The downside of divergent thinkers in the workplace is that they often annoy those with whom they work. The ideas generated by the trait of *originality* could be interpreted by supervisors and coworkers as too unrealistic or too abstract. Many neurotypical coworkers complain that a divergent thinker's *fluency* causes all sorts of issues. I commonly hear that my clients are overloading people with information, proposing too many ideas, and asking too many questions. *Flexibility* in the office (especially in leaders) can be interpreted as not sticking to one idea, ambivalence, or faltering, rather than being seen as possibility thinkers that are able to adapt to a variety of options. My clients who find themselves in the molasses swamp of *elaboration*—getting stuck in all the details and planning in order to be extremely careful—test the patience of their coworkers and employers who just want them to complete their tasks.

Dancing through a Minefield

If you tend to lean on your divergent thinking patterns, you need to be aware of and understand the cognitive errors that you may be prone to make, or you will find yourself dancing through a minefield. One wrong dance step and you lose a leg—or, more practically, a job.

Watch for these common rabbit holes in your divergent thinking.

1. Using Only Divergent Thinking

I was working with a pastor, Paul, who gave beautiful sermons. His congregants would approach him after church and tell him how his words blessed them and challenged them to grow. Behind the scenes, though, his family and staff were very frustrated with his seeming inability to complete the sermon in a timely fashion. Lovingly, they tried to create structure and deadlines for him to follow. It didn't work. And you can guess why. Paul had a strong affinity for divergent thinking. He loved the part of the sermon preparation that involved exploring the texts, reading commentaries, and reflecting on the meaning. That's the divergent stuff. Creating the outline, committing to a focus, choosing what to omit, and sticking with all of his decisions have to do with the less fun and less interesting convergent process.

Let's face it. Those of us with ADHD use divergent thinking patterns because they are more interesting and fun, but we need to balance ourselves by using convergent thinking too. Both convergent and divergent thinking are important for creative problem solving and project planning—which means we should have time set aside for each. The real challenge is to know when to switch gears from our natural divergent track to thinking convergently.

2. Being Interested Only in Big Challenges

It was the most painful piano recital I have ever attended. My client Mark, a very-smart-but-hides-it-well type of student, sat at the piano to play Pachelbel's "Canon in D," a common song for piano students. He began his senior recital with the familiar melody, then stopped and started over again. And stopped. And started again. It was the clunkiest version of the song that I have ever heard. It was like we were witnessing him practice the piece instead of perform it. His teacher finally intervened and told him not to start over again but to continue from a certain point in the music. It was dreadful.

Later in the recital, the teacher introduced Mark and explained that he would be playing a piece he had chosen. He sat on the bench and arranged his music. Then, with focused swiftness, he began. His hands fluttered up and down the keyboard with a focused passion. The music was wonderfully complicated, expressive, and technically impeccable. I was transfixed by the music and stunned by the musician.

Afterward, I congratulated him on his playing. He nodded, pleased with himself. "Thanks!" As he showed me the music, he mentioned the name of a Belgian composer that I didn't catch. His sheet was dark with notes and included marks I didn't recognize. "It's New Complexity!" he said. I nodded and was about to ask another question when we were interrupted.

A week later in our session, Mark explained that New Complexity is a type of music that has compositions that are often atonal and highly abstract. New Complexity is most well-known for the use of extraordinarily complex notation, which places serious demands on the performer.

"What about the first piece?" I asked.

"Eh, the teacher made me play it. It's really boring."

At the recital, Mark had made a common cognitive error. Those who use mostly divergent thinking are often drawn to more complex and difficult endeavors because they are interesting The easier tasks, many of them convergent, still need to be completed, but because they seem too easy or boring, those with ADHD will often neglect them.

3. Being in Love with Your Divergent Thinking

"I am the creative. Everyone else needs to do the details," Amelia said. It was true, she was creative. She designed expensive and beautiful jewelry for her shop downtown. "I make everyone else do the grunt work," she joked. Amelia had come to me for coaching about running her business. Her husband didn't want to do it anymore, and she couldn't keep employees for more than three months. She wanted to create her jewelry and also have full decision-making power over her business. But she didn't want to be dragged "into the weeds," as she put it. She wouldn't answer phone calls, was late for appointments, and forgot to pay employees on time. Her store lost business because of her behavior. Her lack of willingness to do any work that required convergent thinking frustrated and confused her employees.

After weeks of talking about convergent and divergent thinking, I gave her direct feedback. "I'm not saying that you have to keep your own books, but you do need to provide direction for people who work for you. And that means you need to spend some time in convergent thinking about your business so you will be able to direct others to know what to do."

Amelia hated that suggestion, and I didn't see her for weeks. She couldn't see that her reluctance to do any convergent thinking caused messes for others to sort out.

4. Being Fixated on Your "Potential"

Twenty-something Juan was a smart and congenial guy. And he was an achiever. He demanded a lot from himself, making rules and setting goals. "But, Doc," I can still hear him say, "I know I can do so much. What is my potential, and how do I know if I'm reaching it?" For him, *potential* became a four-letter word.

Many smart individuals like Juan struggle with the problem of potential. Parents and teachers have told them consistently that they have "so much potential." Their divergent brains dream of opportunities and accomplishments. They know they have a high capacity to succeed yet are confused by their inconsistent achievement. Even after diagnosis, they deny the impact that ADHD has on their performance. Rather than acknowledge the complexity that ADHD adds to any task, they ascribe their struggles to reach their goals as character flaws. They become frustrated and anxious when they are unable to realize their "potential."

Each time a client goes down that road, I ask, "What do you want to do about it?" We then use convergent thinking to make plans to achieve their goals. When we achieve specific goals, we know that we have stepped closer to our ideal "potential." Doing something about our capacity usually involves convergent thinking.

5. Dealing with Imagination Plus Anxiety

Our wonderfully vivid imaginations combine with our anxiety and fears to create monsters—cognitive distortions that torture us. We let the monsters that we create take over our rational thoughts. Because every single client I have ever seen has identified this trap, I will spend the entire next chapter talking about the monsters we create.

6. Having No Patience for Nondivergent Activities

"This shouldn't be so hard," my husband grumbles as he attempts to make an appointment online. His impatience with mundane tasks quickly shifts into irritation and agitation. People with ADHD tend to believe that mundane tasks should be quick and simple, so they resent it when those tasks take time and energy. Their impatient, emotional responses bubble up from their divergent thinking pattern and aren't useful in the moment.

7. Creating Rube Goldberg Machines

A Rube Goldberg machine, named after American cartoonist Rube Goldberg, is a machine intentionally designed to perform a simple task in an indirect and overly complicated way. My children loved their middle school project of a creative Rube Goldberg machine. It captured their imagination. That's all fine for creative fun, but ADHD adults make the cognitive error of creating these machines in their daily lives rather than keeping to simple methods.

Many adults with whom I work unconsciously create convoluted ways of completing a task while exerting maximum effort. For example, Maria wanted to clean up her kitchen—to do the dishes and declutter the counters. In order to do that, she reasoned that she needed to first clean out all of the cupboards and drawers. She loaded her counter with baking pans, cookie sheets, measuring cups, and mixing bowls as she removed items from each cupboard. Then, looking at the mess, she decided that she needed something to motivate her to complete the task. Listening to *The Office* on her iPad sounded perfect. But before she could do that, she would have to find her password to the account because one of her children had accidentally logged her out of it. She called her husband at work and asked, "Do you have the password for Netflix? I need to clean the kitchen."

That is an ADHD Rube Goldberg machine. Most of the time these machines are overly complicated, are distracting, and just don't work. Maria's simple task was to do the dishes and clean off the counters. Instead of converging the task and just doing it, Maria spent the day preparing to do the work, making the project lengthier and more complicated than it needed to be.

Apply the KISS principle whenever you can. When I catch myself making a Rube Goldberg machine, I say, "Keep it simple and straightforward." I take a deep breath and slide into a convergent mode.

8. Getting Stuck in Problem Finding

Given our tendency toward imagination and expansive thinking, those of us who depend on divergent thinking are problem-finding geniuses! Kristine can tell you all the ways that something will go wrong with her own personal game of "What if." Although this game is her attempt at planning in the divergent thinking pattern, she is actually getting stuck in the problem-finding stage. Her brain circles the drain of finding more and more problems to consider, and soon she gives up, feeling anxious, sad, or just tired. Problem finding is only the first stage. Eventually, she needs to shift from problem finding to convergent problem solving.

Problem solving is where we narrow choices and choose a direction. Making a decision feels very challenging when we try to rely only on divergent thinking. Many of my clients complain, "There are so many options. How do I know the best one?" When they use divergent thinking, all ideas are treated equally regardless of context or applicability. Projected goals, rules, directions, or criteria are often neglected as divergent thinkers tackle a problem from multiple perspectives to find original solutions. But decision-making takes both divergent thinking and convergent thinking.

9. Not Monitoring Your Divergent Pattern

Emily took a quick bathroom break from painting her basement with her husband. While in the bathroom, she flossed her teeth. She looked down at Maggie, who was staring at her with the adoring eyes of a dog in love with its human. She sat on the floor to cuddle her bundle of cuteness. Her phone buzzed with a TikTok from her sister. She responded with a "haha" tap back. Then she checked her email and saw Target's promotional ad. She thought she should probably go to Target that day to purchase some of those sale items.

Her husband walked into the bathroom with a paintbrush still in hand, paint smeared on his pants, and asked, "Are you okay?" Emily looked up from where she still sat on the bathroom floor. "It's been forty-five minutes," he said.

This is the most common error of all—we pop down a rabbit hole and forget where we are supposed to be. We need to maintain a meta-awareness of which type of thinking we are using and question if it is effective in the moment.

What are your most common divergent thinking errors? Instead of wringing your hands each time you make one of these errors, learn to spot them as soon as they occur and shift your thinking and your actions.

Learning to Shift

Imagine your supervisor gives you the task of organizing a fundraiser event. You start by brainstorming creative ideas: happy hours with famous speakers, a tropical island–themed night, a fashion show, a 5K run, a silent auction, or a black-and-white party. From there, you move into convergent thinking, evaluate the options, and settle on the ones that work best for your constituents.

That's how successful projects should progress. Too often project managers rely on one type of thinking for too long. Many books have been written cautioning the reader not to be so eager to pin down a plan, which doesn't allot time for imaginations to run wild. Those of us who prefer divergent thinking have the opposite issue. We love the exploration of ideas so much that we forget to shift to the convergent process. To paraphrase the book of Ecclesiastes, there is a time to generate ideas and a time for evaluating them and moving forward.

I watch as many of my clients attempt to do both types of thinking at once, but they only end up frustrated with themselves. Trying to think both divergently and convergently at the same time is counterproductive. Mixing the two is like putting your foot on the gas at the same time as the brake. Jillian, a young professional, has learned this well. Each day at work, she sorts her tasks into two groups. "There are tasks that are only convergent—returning emails, finishing budgets, and stuff like that. But the social media work that I do for my organization is fun and mostly divergent. I save those tasks like treats for the end of my day." Jillian has learned that while both types of thinking are necessary for success, it's smarter to identify and separate them, sorting them in a way that will allow for the most productive day possible for her.

Monitor your thinking closely. (Some of my clients set timers for the two different types of thinking.) Ask yourself, "What is my goal for this part of the task?" If the answer is getting the laundry done, don't shift to divergent thinking and redecorate the laundry room. Instead, set a timer and tell yourself that you will spend fifteen minutes in convergent thinking while you perform this task.

Divergent thinking and rabbit holes aren't your enemies. They are forms of thinking that allow you to have big ideas and make stunning connections. Learning to manage the tension between the desire for divergent thinking and the practical need for convergent thinking will help you become more effective in your life and help you better manage some of your ADHD tendencies.

5

The Monsters We Face

Seven-year-old Annie studied me while her mom explained why they needed help. "We are having all kinds of issues. She won't sleep in her bed, and she won't be in a room by herself."

I nodded and jotted a few notes, asking questions about any recent trauma or significant changes. There weren't any.

The mother went on to explain how Annie would even ask one of her twin two-year-old siblings to accompany her to the bathroom because she could not be alone. "This is causing all kinds of potty accidents," she said.

I was impressed by how together this mom was. She was frustrated with her child's behavior, but for a woman with four children ages seven and under, she seemed to be calm and very thoughtful about how she parented in spite of this challenge. She was willing to do whatever she needed to problem-solve this.

I turned to the small blonde girl with impossibly large, dark-brown eyes. "Do you know why you don't want to be alone?"

Annie cautiously nodded. "Monsters."

"Oh," I said quite seriously. I leaned toward her and confided, "I understand the monster problem."

The monster problem—in whatever form it takes—is common among children with ADHD, as they tend to have brilliant imaginations. When they get anxious, their anxieties get trapped in their inventive brains as they try to understand something outside their frame of reference. Those inventive brains can concoct a story that causes the anxiety to turn into full-blown fear.

Since children's life experiences are more limited than those of adults, they don't understand how to process their anxieties— much less even know that's how to label the tumultuous feeling inside their little bodies. So, in a sense, Annie's monsters were real. They represented all the things in her world that were overwhelming and not understandable to her as a first grader. And these things don't have to be big traumas. They can be as small as missing recess because you were talking in class or being embarrassed by a teacher asking you a question that you don't know the answer to.

Annie's monsters seemed to emerge when she was tired and not distracted by activities, so it made sense that they appeared regularly at bedtime. Like with many adults with ADHD, her monsters didn't come out during the day simply because she was busy and not looking for them. She did what so many kids and adults who have ADHD do—instead of releasing the day's thoughts, concerns, and worries toward the evening, she would examine and obsess on them to the extreme.

"Yep," I told her while she sized me up. "I had a monster problem too when I was your age. I used to try to leap onto my bed so that whatever was under it couldn't catch my feet. Although I never saw them in the basement, I was pretty sure there were monsters there too."

She gave me a hearty nod. She understood that well.

"What have you tried to do to keep them away?"

She shrugged. "Nothing."

Like so many people dealing with anxiety and fear, Annie forgot—or didn't even know—that she could do something about them. She had more authority over fear and anxiety than she understood. Knowing that Annie was listening, I turned to address her mom and said in my most adult, clinical-sounding voice, "Have you tried monster spray?"

Fortunately, the with-it mother kept pace and replied in a steady tone, "No, but we could try it."

I turned to Annie again. "I don't think you can kill the monsters. But you can keep them away." I explained how the monster spray works. Even though it smells good to us, monsters think the spray stinks and want to stay away. I described how skunks spray a terrible smell to get other animals and humans to stay away. Annie wrinkled her nose, so I knew she'd smelled a skunk before.

Again, her mom had my back and said to her daughter, "You know how I put peppermint oil on cotton balls in the basement to keep spiders away? It's like that."

"Would you be willing to use the monster spray?" I asked. "It sounds like your mom already has the ingredients for it."

Annie seemed skeptical but nodded slowly.

Addressing her mother again in my professional tone, I gave the instructions for making the monster spray: twelve drops of peppermint oil and five ounces of water in a glass spray bottle. Mom nodded seriously, taking a pen and paper to make note of the recipe. She and I spent the rest of the session covering other parenting topics while Annie played on the floor, building a house with some Magna-Tiles.

As her mom and I were wrapping up the session, Annie's small voice interrupted, "What if it doesn't work?"

"It will," I reassured her. "But there's a different spray recipe for problems with the hairy kinds of monsters. That spray uses lavender." I paused a moment, looking out the window as though thinking. I turned back to her and said, "Oh, and one more thing.

Your little brothers may have a monster problem too. Would you be willing to help them? Maybe share your spray and explain things to them?" This time Annie nodded with the type of pride that an older sibling has when asked to share her expertise.

The next day, her mom left a voice message for me. "The monster spray worked! Annie slept in her bed, took a shower by herself, and didn't have any crying fits."

Reminding Annie that she had authority over her fears helped her keep them at bay.

Adults Have Monsters Too

When I shared Annie's story with another client who has high anxiety, she understood Annie's plight all too well. Elizabeth, a young professional in the nonprofit world, explained, "When my husband is traveling, I won't shower without locking the door, and I won't go in our basement at all. Even when he is home, I hate the furnace room of the basement so much that I refuse to go in there."

Elizabeth is an example of how our ADHD-related anxieties leach into our imaginations. Although rationally she knows that the furnace room in her basement isn't haunted, she has so many generalized fears that her imagination goes wild with possibilities.

Renaissance philosopher Michel de Montaigne seemed to know something about the imagined monsters we face when he wrote, "He who fears he shall suffer, already suffers what he fears."[1] In other words, when someone worries that something will happen, their mind and body are already experiencing the very thing they are fearing as though it is currently taking place.

Just like Annie, adults with ADHD have monsters too. Two of our natural ADHD tendencies—divergent thinking patterns and lack of emotional regulation—collide to create vicious and scary monsters from everyday occurrences.

Monster in the Spice Aisle

Ben described a recent grocery shopping event. "I needed to find bay leaves, but I was already dreading it because I hate the spice aisle. It's so overwhelming. As I followed the overhead signs, the questions began. 'What if I can't find bay leaves? Am I looking for a box or a bottle? What does a bay leaf look like? What will my wife use them for anyway? Could I buy a substitute? How would I know what a substitute for bay leaves would be? Do we really need them? I've never seen her use that spice before.'"

You can already detect Ben's divergent thinking style as he relayed this experience. Remember from chapter 4 that divergent thinking is the tendency to explore many directions of a thought in a spontaneous, free-flowing, nonlinear manner. Ben's mind drove past the simple task of finding the bay leaves to the unlikely event of not finding what he needed to wondering if bay leaves are even necessary. This is where neurotypicals can be confused by observing the ADHD process. "Just find the bay leaves," they may be tempted to suggest. It seems absurdly simple—and for non-ADHD folks, it is. But Ben's thoughts fling out in many directions at the same time, causing a cacophony of questions and ideas all at once.

Ben continued his spice-hunt story. "Standing in front of the massive display, I thought, *Why would they organize spice shelves this way? How would I organize them? Why isn't there an employee I can ask? Where did they all go? They need to have more employees here on the weekend.* As he scanned each shelf, everything blended together as though the spices were collaborating against him to hide the bay leaves. Eventually, his emotions swelled and he threw up his hands. "I'm tired of being here. I'm tired *and* stupid. Geesh." Ben left feeling overwhelmed, irritated, and defeated.

The other tendency that creates ADHD monsters is the lack of emotional regulation. Like most people with ADHD, Ben has a very low frustration tolerance. Because his brain confuses little everyday inconveniences with major threats, he can easily escalate a minor irritation into a struggle with a monster frustration. He often becomes completely flooded by a feeling or feelings, making the situation unbearable.

For Ben, the simple task of finding a spice became a crusade. His brain responded as if it were engaged in an attack against real monsters. His breathing sped up; his mind raced. He called this physiological response anxiety. No matter what label we give it—anxiety, fear, worry, stress, or monsters—so many of us with ADHD carry this extra mental load.

Fear is an emotional and physiological response to an imagined or known threat—which means we feel it not only in our minds but also somewhere in our bodies. Some people feel a tightening in their stomach. Some may feel pounding in their chest, pressure in their throat, or even ringing in their ears. Yet for others, there's a lingering apprehension, a dizzying feeling. They carry a chronic sense of worry or tension, the sources of which may be unclear, in their upper back and neck. A client explained, "It's like I'm always waiting for the other shoe to drop. I just know something is going to go wrong. I feel it in my face, a tingling."

Just like Annie's monsters were real because her body thought they were real, so are yours—they just might bear a different name.

Consider Your Monsters

If you have ADHD, you likely have monsters. Naming the beasts you are facing is the first essential step to managing them or banishing them from your life. Naming things is built deep into our subconscious. To name a thing is to acknowledge its existence as separate from everything else that has a name. During early childhood development, as a very young child learns to speak, you can see the relief and delight on their face as they name something. Giving something a name makes it real and able to be communicated about in order to transform its strangeness into familiarity.

Name your monster by addressing your fear. What stresses you out? What makes you feel anxious? What is that thing you worry about? Sometimes your fear is more generalized or nebulous. Do you have a deep fear of being rejected? Are you afraid of not being worthy of love? Of failing? Of being vulnerable? Of not having the support you need? Name it.

"I'm afraid of my child dying," Tanya told me as she was naming her monsters. She had worked through years of infertility and was finally blessed with a beautiful baby girl. The dam to her emotional regulation broke when the new mother held her precious newborn. She had never felt such intense emotions. At the same time, she was willing to die for this person she had just met—and to kill for her. Then she began to wonder, *What would I do if my girl died?*

Her daughter is now eighteen years old, and Tanya still quietly fights the monster each time her daughter leaves the house. "My monster is losing my daughter," she said to me, then tilted her head. "But it makes sense. I love her so intensely, and I have a great imagination that assumes the worst possible outcome. I made a monster."

Where Do Your Monsters Hide?

Ben found one of his monsters in the spice aisle of the supermarket. How about yours? Do they hide in new situations? In social situations? In your email folder? On your phone? Locating where your monsters hide is a way to anticipate and confront them.

I find that I avoid listening to messages on my phone for the simple reason that I don't know what will happen. I get overwhelmed at even the thought of listening to unexpected calls and then having to follow up. When I see messages on my phone, I can feel the beast menacingly peeking at me. So I grab a cup of tea and relax, telling myself that I can face whatever is in that voicemail box.

When do your monsters appear? For Annie, they seemed to appear mostly in the evening when she was tired. For Elizabeth, they appeared to her when her husband left for business travel. When do the monsters affect you? When you walk into a room of unknown people? When you face an unexpected or expected confrontation? When you do something new?

Finding Your Monster Spray

The purpose of any good monster spray is to remind a person that they have more authority over their anxieties, worries, stress, or fears than they realize. How can you remind yourself that you have more power over the racing thoughts, foreboding images, and torturous specters than you understand?

One way to do this is to notice where in your body you feel your anxiety, worry, or fear. Your brain is telling your body that it believes you are in some sort of peril. Some people feel their stress monster in their chest. Do you feel your heart pounding against your rib cage? Do you have chest pain? Do you have shortness of breath or sensations of being smothered? Some feel the anxiety in their head. They feel unsteady, flushed, or light-headed. Many people feel it in their stomach, experiencing nausea or abdominal distress. One of my daughters experienced intestinal issues when she was nervous before a sporting event. She sat quietly in our minivan, fretting while her gaseous stench gave her away. I would sniff and then name it for her. "So you're nervous about this game." Learn to listen to and respond to your body's signals.

Henry, an analyst, explained in a session, "When I wonder if I'm feeling fear or anxiety, I've learned to check in with my body. It is then that I realize I'm breathing like someone is chasing me." He showed me his posture when that happens—hunched over as if to protect his vital organs. "When I recognize this, I straighten up my body, breathing more slowly. It's like I can feel my brain chemistry change along with my posture." Another client realized that he felt intense stress while at his desk at work. Once he noticed it, he said, "I learned to relax each muscle in my face and then moved down my body, relaxing each muscle." The secret to this strategy is cuing your body to relax so that the brain can follow. Take slow, deep breaths, changing posture so that your back is straight, or distract your mind by watching that funny talking-dog video on your phone. Teach your body to relax, telling your brain that it is not in danger.

People find great ways of managing their mental monsters. A midlife professional client learned that his ADHD brain often thinks that situations are significant threats when they are not, so he has developed a way to bring himself back to the center. "When I feel threatened, vulnerable, or insecure, I repeat to myself, 'There is no danger; there is no threat.' From there, the discomfort lessens." Another client asks herself, "Is this a big-deal bucket item, or does it go in the small-deal bucket? Although it usually feels big, I try to verify that it actually belongs in the small-deal bucket. So I change how I think about it and move it to the appropriate 'bucket.'" The secret to this type of monster spray is the capacity to discern a real threat from a smaller sense of discomfort.

One of my clients, a therapist, went ahead and made her monster spray. Literally. "I love the smell of lemongrass, so I thought, 'Why not?'" She describes a learned sense of release when she sprays it. "I relax, and then I am open for discovery and adventure." Her clients now associate the bright green color and lemony-citrus smell with her office. "Some days, now that I am not working with as much ADHD type of anxiety, I forget to spray it, and my clients will ask for it. Maybe it has become a monster spray for other people too."

After the spice-aisle incident, Ben learned that his formula was slowing his movements while breathing slowly. Elizabeth found that she could talk to her husband on the phone and then listen to calming music as she went about her evening activities. For Tanya's fear of losing her daughter, she realized that her recipe was simple.

She caught the dreadful thought and called it out for what it was. "I have this fear because I love deeply and am very imaginative."

Our divergent thinking patterns give us astonishing imaginative and cognitive power. But we can mismanage our thinking ability when we create monsters out of ordinary items and events.

Find your monster spray recipe and manage your monsters with the Peter Parker/Spider-Man principle, a proverb by comic-book writer Stan Lee: "With great power there must also come great responsibility." Retrain your divergent thinking when you are tempted to let fear take over your life.

6

Malicious Motivation

If you have ADHD, there are several reasons why it is difficult for you to accomplish things, and none of them have to do with laziness or not trying hard enough. Most researchers agree that the ADHD brain is wired toward having low motivation for everyday tasks. Dr. Russell Barkley, an internationally recognized authority on this topic, explains that ADHD is more about loss of interest and motivation than attention and concentration. The key to getting things done is to see the emotions involved and learn to redirect them.[1]

Motivation Is about Emotion

Joseph LeDoux's book *The Emotional Brain* emphasizes that emotions—mostly unconscious emotions—are powerful and critically important motivators of human thought (not just ADHD thought) and actions. His book introduced me to the protective nature of our amygdala and how it wordlessly sounds the alarm to the rest of the reactive limbic system (see illustration in chapter 3).[2] It changed how I thought about emotions and motivation.

Then along came psychiatrist William Dodson, who built on the notion of how important emotions are to the ADHD process. After specializing in treating adults with ADHD for more than a quarter of a century, he has determined that their motivation is affected by two aspects of ADHD: an interest-based nervous system and emotional hyperarousal.

An *interest-based nervous system* implies that we are motivated by our level of interest in something rather than its importance and priority. In other words, importance, rewards, and consequences don't spur us into action.

"That's exactly it!" David said when I explained how motivation works with ADHD. "I have *always* been able to do anything I wanted as long as I could get excited about it." He and so many of my clients are relieved to have their interest-based motivation understood.

Emotional hyperarousal refers to the intensity of emotion that people with ADHD feel. We have passionate thoughts and emotions that are more intense than those of the average person. As I discussed in chapter 3, our highs are higher and our lows are lower. Our intense moods are triggered by events and perceptions and fortunately usually resolve very quickly. These moods are normal in every way except for their intensity.

Subconscious emotions are powerful and complex and affect how we motivate ourselves. Especially for those of us with ADHD, the stronger the emotional push, the more likely we will be engaged. Many of us unconsciously call on the emotional part of our brain to initiate a task, especially a task we find tedious, uninteresting, or routine.

It is easy to understand why getting stuff done when we have ADHD is so darn difficult. Our inconsistent interest and big emotions work against us.

Using emotion to motivate ourselves is tricky business, and we can easily end up in a ditch after using it. When the emotion becomes too much, the angry neighbor arrives, and feelings of being overwhelmed set in. Because it is so difficult to motivate ourselves, we resort to some dirty tricks to get things done.

In this chapter, you'll learn how my clients Charlotte, David, Claudia, Christopher, and Bob have fallen into common ADHD motivational traps. As you read, identify when you have used these malicious motivational tricks on yourself: avoidance, anxiety, procrastination, anger, shame, and self-loathing.[3]

Avoidance: You'd Rather Be Doing Something Else

Although Claudia had a very important work project that was due, she decided to repaint her bathroom instead. She dove into redecorating websites at her office and sorted through paint chips at night. "At least my bathroom will look nice," she said. "I have been wanting to do that for a while." Claudia didn't want to face the work project, so she let herself become distracted by another less urgent task. She was using a sneaky emotional and motivational trick called avoidance.

We use the avoidance tactic to motivate ourselves to do other things instead of the important task before us. Avoidance lets us feel productive by accomplishing something—even though it is not what needs to be done.

When we don't want to think about the task that makes us emotionally uncomfortable or even anxious, we temporarily shift our attention. This misdirection soothes our twitchy limbic system, calming our anxiety. A college student, Charlotte, confessed with a wry smile, "My sock drawer is usually very clean around exam time." Instead of writing her papers and studying for finals, she looks around her messy room and decides to organize her socks. "I feel so good thinking about my color-coded sock drawer that I forget how gross school is making me feel." Charlotte avoided the bad feelings that she associated with school by completing a task that she could feel good about.

Avoidance is driven by a variety of thoughts and habits. We avoid tasks or put them off because we do not believe we'll enjoy doing them or we fear that we won't do them well. We may also use avoidance when we are confused by the complexity of a task (such as filing our taxes) or when we're overly distracted or fatigued. And sometimes we use avoidance despite our best intentions.

Christopher set out to be more productive in his life. Each night he would create a list of tasks for the following day. I asked him, "Does that method work well for you?" His first response was an enthusiastic "Yes!" Then he paused. "I'm not sure that it is working. I never really get to the list that I wrote." Christopher described how he dreaded getting out of bed in the morning because he knew that the items he listed the night before should be done. When he finally faced his day, he avoided completing his list and did other things instead. His attempt at being productive and making the list was actually perpetuating his avoidance pattern.

Our divergent thinking may work against us when we are trying to get things done. In divergent thinking, everything has the same level of importance. I accidentally slip into an avoidance strategy when items pop into my head as I work on a task. The new thoughts seem just as important, and I am tempted to follow them down the rabbit hole. Sometimes when I suspect that I may be struggling with avoidance, I shift into a just-do-it, convergent thinking mode, but if I can't, I take a quick break to analyze my thoughts. I look at my list and ask myself, "Why did I think this task was important?" I try to retrace my thoughts to understand why I would prioritize a specific task. Then I ask questions to test my thinking about prioritization. "Is there a due date? What will happen if I don't complete this task? Have I scheduled a time to complete it?" Usually I will feel dread and argue with myself. "But I don't *want* to do it." That is usually how I know that I need to address my avoidance.

Anxiety: The Tyranny of the Urgent

Prioritizing tasks and knowing what to do first is difficult for those of us with ADHD, so we rely on anxious feelings to tell us what needs to be done. "I can feel myself getting worked up about doing my billing," Bob, a media consultant, says. "I try to invoice my clients by the third of each month for the previous month. I catch myself watching the calendar, feeling nervous and agitated about the upcoming task." Unconsciously, Bob is building on the feeling of anxiety to create a sense of anticipation and urgency for doing the task. He is increasing his motivation as he worries and frets. "I worry that I will forget it, even though it's on my calendar, or mess it up somehow, even though it's easy to do," he explains. Bob's basic motivation is a faint flame reminding him that he should get to a task. He pours gasoline—anxious thoughts—on that flame, and *poof*! Big motivation!

Claudia, a middle-aged professional and mother, explains that she uses anxiety to accomplish mundane things. She finds herself anxious about locking her car doors. *I need to remember to lock my car*, she thinks, and then her thoughts race on. *I need to listen for the beep. What if I double-clicked my key fob and it actually unlocked the car? Someone could steal my stuff. What is in my car? Oh, my son's iPad. I don't want that stolen. He would be so sad, and I can't buy a new one right now. Lock car. Lock car. Lock car.* Although anxiety focuses her attention on completing a simple task, it is not a reliable system. Sometimes the anxious feeling won't go away, she says. "I get all the way up to my office and then go back down because I am so concerned that I forgot." She tells me that usually she has already locked her car.

David, a twenty-something young professional, uses anxiety to make sure he is on time. He arrives at my office ten minutes early as if he just finished a race. Everything in his body seems to scream, "I made it! I'm here! Let's get started!" His leg bounces as he sits in the waiting room, and his eyes dart about the area. He appears to be on high alert.

"I don't know how or why it started," he says. He explains that he grew up in Singapore and wasn't overly focused on being on time. "But after college in the US, I have a preoccupation with not being late. I will not allow myself to be late. Lunch with a friend? I'll be ten minutes early. A job interview? If I'm not there at least fifteen minutes beforehand, I feel panicked. I feel compelled to be prompt. But when does having a propensity for timeliness turn into something more? Am I neurotic?"

David used his emotional hyperarousal system to govern his timeliness. It is another way that those of us with ADHD manage ourselves with anxiety. Our error is to use this strategy as our primary motivation for action. In order to go places and get things done, we find we are "urgency junkies," having become overly reliant on the emotionally salient feelings of the urgent. We use anxiety to move us into action and to increase our performance. "I like to call it just-in-time planning," Charlotte says jokingly, then frowns. "Actually, it's exhausting."

Though we may be successful in our reliance on a sense of urgency, our results become inconsistent over time and across domains. As it is with each of our dirty emotional tricks, the drawback is that motivating ourselves with anxiety is exhausting. When our intense anxiety gets too high, we are likely to avoid a task or shut down and not do anything at all.

Procrastination: Dodging Bullets

Everyone puts off things sometimes, but those with ADHD chronically avoid specific tasks and deliberately look for distractions. Here's how we use procrastination to motivate our emotionally focused brains.

Procrastination begins with avoidance thoughts such as, *I don't feel like doing that right now.* We imagine a magical time when we will feel intrinsically motivated to do that task. And we wait. And we wait until we can wait no longer. Then with the quickly approaching deadline, a wicked wave of anxiety, fear, or anger pushes us into action. We complete the task with only minutes to spare.

This is our genius tactic for getting things done that combines the two previous techniques: avoidance and anxiety.

Many of us have made a habit of last-minute work to experience euphoria's rush at seemingly having overcome the odds. My college-age clients often brag, "This twenty-five-page paper was assigned at the beginning of the semester. I did it in ten hours! I barely ate or used the bathroom, and I pulled an all-nighter!" Their faces are energized with the thrill of dodging a bullet. Right now it feels like a high for them. They motivated themselves to complete an overwhelming task by using procrastination and the feeling of intense emotion that comes from it.

Many of my clients believe that they need to work under pressure in order to perform well, convincing themselves that they do their best work when they procrastinate. Research shows that is generally not the case, again indicating that our performance and productivity suffer under such pressure.

Procrastinating Because of Perfectionism

Some of us who procrastinate do so because we are secretly perfectionists.

I was driving home from the zoo with my two young children, who had just fallen asleep in the back of my SUV, and I started to make a list of what I needed to do when I arrived at home. "Today's show is about the poverty of perfectionism," the radio host said, interrupting my thoughts.

"That's definitely not me. I've never done anything right," I muttered to myself and reached for the radio dial. I was messy and not detail oriented. My work was always lacking and never finished.

But before I could change the station, the host said, "And if you are a true perfectionist, you just said that you couldn't be because you've never done anything perfect in your life."

Wait, what? I had never considered that I could be a perfectionist. I was shocked. As the radio announcer went on to describe *me*,

I pulled into a parking lot under a shade tree. While my daughters finished their nap, I learned that I was, indeed, a perfectionist.

Perfectionists are quick to find fault in themselves and others and are overly critical of mistakes. Because I know that I want to be able to do things right, I procrastinate out of my fear of criticism, failure, or rejection. Procrastinating perfectionists often feel that it may be psychologically more acceptable to never tackle a job than to face the possibility of not doing it well. For me, perfectionism was the belief that I would never live up to a (mostly unconscious) standard that I had set for myself. Self-condemnation kept me from starting a task until I absolutely had to. Although it would be years before I understood how ADHD emotions perpetuated perfectionism and procrastination, I knew that I needed to change something.

I am not alone in this tendency. It runs rampant in the ADHD world. In order to change that trajectory, fellow ADHD perfectionists need to recognize their pattern of perfection and that it is not helping them.

I haven't completely let go of the shame of being imperfect, but I confront it daily. Instead of procrastinating on writing an article because I know that it will not be good enough, I coach myself by saying, "Let's just write a quick draft and see what happens." Then after I write the draft and perfectionism tells me once again that it isn't good enough, I confront it by saying, "Read it aloud. Let's make sure it sounds right." And so it goes—perfection accuses me, and then I reason with it.

Talking with Your Past, Present, and Future Self

I learned that each time I procrastinate, my future self pays the price. So many times, I found myself angry with a past version of myself who procrastinated on a task, calling my past self stupid, lazy, and other names. But scolding myself didn't help me to stop procrastinating. I needed to change my approach. So I decided to try to help my future self instead of hurting her. I understood that my decisions in the moment would help determine whether my future self would be more likely or less likely to experience success. I could treat my future self with kindness by taking care of tasks that needed to be done or with cruelty by willfully procrastinating.

I began imagining having a conversation with my future self. I imagined the version of me who would wake up in my bed tomorrow. I needed to remind myself that I like this person and want the best for her. From there I began to think about how the things I do, say, eat, and experience would change the way my future self felt about waking up tomorrow. Would my future self wake up tired because I stayed up bingeing on Netflix? Would my future self struggle to shake off indigestion because I chose to eat pizza even though I am lactose intolerant? Would my early-morning future self have to worry about being unprepared because I didn't feel like selecting an outfit and packing up my computer and papers in my work bag the night before? I began asking my future self a specific question: "What would help you have a great morning?" And it worked! When I answered that question in specific ways, I saw a decline in my nightly procrastination immediately.

David was just beginning to use the future-self technique as he was thinking about a computer-programming assignment that was due on Tuesday. "I want to get it done on Saturday." He sighed. "I say that, but I always wait until the last minute."

"What time do you think Saturday David will start working on it?" I asked.

"Probably around two."

"What does Friday David need to do to support Saturday David?" He began, "He shouldn't stay up late gaming." Then he stopped. He seemed surprised by a thought he'd just had. "You know, I could look over the assignment on Friday, write down any questions, and pose them to my study group today! That way I will be ready to complete the assignment on Saturday."

A week later, when I asked about his assignment, David was pleased to tell me that although he had completed it on Sunday, not Saturday, he still felt successful. "I had never considered helping my future self and setting him up for success." The reason he couldn't follow his exact plan for completing his task on Saturday was because there were complications he didn't understand about the assignment. Instead of letting this setback defeat or derail him, he thought about how he could support the Sunday version of himself by completing what he could on Saturday and then making a plan to address the complications the next day. "I still finished it two days before it was due," he said. Applying this new attitude of being considerate and supportive of his future self, he didn't slip into his old familiar pattern of ignoring the assignment until the deadline.

Being grateful to our past selves is helpful as we encourage growth and change in our patterns of procrastination. I was taking Christmas decorations out of the closet when my teenage daughter stepped into the room to witness me turn around, raise my palm, and slap the air. "What was that?" she asked, looking at me with the "why are my parents so weird?" expression that she frequently wears.

Her apparent judgment didn't dampen my delight. I replied, "I was high-fiving my past self! She is so organized. She did a great job putting away the boxes last year!"

To neurotypicals, this strategy may sound ridiculous. But for those of us with ADHD and limited access to our prefrontal cortex, this strategy turns what would be a convergent thinking activity into an imaginative, divergent one.

Anger: Getting Mad Moves You to Action

Motivating ourselves with anger can help us do that stupid little task that has been haunting us for days or months. The flare of anger makes us feel strong and pushes us to do what we want to get done.

"Stupid winter, stupid weather, stupid Michigan," Bob muttered as he prepared the garage for winter. The weather had already turned cold, and snow was on its way. He needed an hour to put away warm-weather things, like garden hoses and deck furniture, and prepare his snowblower for the inevitable future snowstorms. Bob was surprised to find that he had used anger as a sneaky motivational trick. "I didn't consider my flare-up of anger as trying to motivate myself," he said later, "but I had to get mad to clean the garage."

Sometimes we learn the effectiveness of using anger as motivation because other people were angry with us. David told me about how his mother used to scream at him. "She was easily angered by my behavior," he explained. He had worked with a counselor to realize that as a result, he learned to be motivated when someone was yelling at him. "When no one else was around to yell at me, I learned to yell at myself." If there was something for him to do at work, he would muster all the anger at himself or others that he could in order to complete the task. "I'm just so tired," he told me. "But the only way I know how to get myself moving is with anger."

There are several problems with using anger to motivate ourselves. In addition to being exhausting, anger didn't help David think more clearly. Instead, the result was just the opposite. It clouded his thinking and judgment. Anger only gave him the emotional impetus to move.

Though it can be tempting, even exciting, to use anger to motivate ourselves, research suggests that persistent anger for prolonged periods of time is detrimental to our productivity and our health. In Bob's case, he wasn't the only one in the garage—his son was there to help, forced to endure Bob's crankiness. Instead of Bob creating a positive memory with his child, his son was affected by his malicious self-motivation, making the task miserable for him.

Shame and Self-Loathing: Motivation through Disgust at Yourself

The last dirty emotional tricks that those of us with ADHD use to accomplish tasks are even more dastardly and exhausting than the previous ones. We turn to shame and self-loathing as strategies when the previous ones fail. These tools require us to increase the frequency and duration of our intense emotions. Shame and self-loathing aren't turned on briefly like the previous tricks of avoidance, anxiety, procrastination, and anger. Instead, these dirty emotional tricks often act like chronic inflammation, a constant irritation to our emotional sense of well-being.

Unhealthy shame is different from healthy shame. When we feel guilty because we did something to hurt someone, that is the healthy version of shame. It's telling us that we did something against our value system. It's a signal to change our direction, make amends, and rectify the situation.

Unhealthy shame, on the other hand, is when we allow ourselves to be defined by a weakness or something we have no control over. According to Brené Brown, a researcher at the University of Houston, shame is an "intensely painful feeling or experience of believing that we are flawed and therefore unworthy of love and belonging."[4] She explains that shame is an emotion that affects all of us and profoundly shapes the way we interact in the world.

Many of my clients use shame to motivate themselves to accomplish their daily tasks. Claudia realized that she used shame to motivate herself at work and at home, always trying to prove her worth to her supervisor and herself. She says, "To start a project I've been putting off, I'll imagine how disappointed my supervisor will be if I don't finish it in time. She'll realize that she shouldn't even have given me this job in the first place."

Charlotte also relies on shaming herself. "I only have one chance to give my kids a good childhood. I have to get it right or I'll screw them up for the rest of their lives." She berates herself when the house isn't kept tidy or if she messes up the family schedule, which is filled with kids' activities. By focusing on her flaws and imperfections, this busy mom uses shame to keep up the momentum in her life.

In using shame to motivate ourselves, we tend to rehearse the ways that we are incomplete, damaged, incompetent, weak, and stupid. Taking those broken beliefs, we challenge ourselves to prove that we are not those things. It is a sucker's game. Though a task may be completed eventually, we experience no win because we still feel exhausted and emptied by the shame we carry.

Sometimes the habit of motivating ourselves with shame turns into a steady practice of self-loathing. Commonly, it manifests itself through us belittling or undervaluing ourselves. Disguised as discipline, self-loathing is done for the sake of teaching ourselves a lesson, to motivate ourselves to "just do better."

David explained how he used self-loathing to improve his financial situation. "I hated the fact that I didn't have more money. I couldn't blame anyone but myself. I hated feeling like a loser. That belief drove me each day." His self-loathing worked. He did make more money. But he suffered in other areas of his life as a result, including family life, and he was left with more self-loathing.

Confronting Harmful Motivation

As you wake up each day, imagine that your life battery is fully charged. You are hopeful and are ready to take on the day. But as the day goes by, your charge will slowly decline. Each poor emotional motivational technique you use drains your battery rapidly and leaves you feeling physically and emotionally exhausted. This is how malicious motivation is costly to you.

Address the emotional manipulations you use to motivate yourself. Breaking the pattern of using them takes commitment to retraining your brain. It is going to take work to learn new habits of thinking, but you will be able to do it.

1. Begin by assessing your current usage. Which emotional tricks are you using to motivate yourself? When do you tend to use them? How do you use them? What are the

negative effects of using avoidance, anxiety, procrastination, anger, shame, and self-loathing in your life?

2. Try this experiment: Set an alarm for an hour from now. When the alarm goes off, write down an emotional trick you used or were tempted to use during that time, whether at work or at home. Set the alarm again and repeat. Look for patterns in your thinking.

3. Commit to restricting the use of these destructive mental habits and motivations. If you are like I was, struggling with a sense of self-worth, you may want to talk to a professional. A coach or counselor who is specifically trained in the area of ADHD can help you acknowledge, address, and stop using these strategies.

4. Enlist the support of a trusted confidant. Ask your spouse or a friend to give you feedback when they see you using one of these tactics. Teach them to ask you a question that will alert you to your error, such as, "Are you using a malicious motivational tactic right now?"

5. Learn new tricks. As you confront and slap away your impulses to use avoidance, anxiety, procrastination, anger, shame, and self-loathing to motivate yourself, you will want to reframe how you can inspire yourself to move forward. You can even employ two aspects of ADHD: an interest-based nervous system and emotional hyperarousal.

Now What?

It is reasonable to ask, "If I can't use these strategies, then what can I do to motivate myself?" Each of us needs to find our own successful strategies. What works for me may not work for you. You need to create your individual "owner's manual" to spark interest that leads to action. The rest of this book will stimulate and guide your thinking as you do this.

Solving Motivational Murders

"I know what I want to do, but I can't seem to do it," my clients often say during their first appointments with me. "And I don't know why." They are talking about the lack of the "just do it" command button that most neurotypical people seem to have in their heads but that my clients feel is missing. And with no "just do it" button, those with ADHD experience the act of tackling a to-do list in a very different way than those around them.

In the previous chapter, we discussed how we use malicious emotional techniques to wrangle our big ADHD emotions into motivating ourselves to accomplish tasks. There are a few other challenges that kill or mess with our motivation, which is affected by how we experience time and our fascination with shiny, fun tasks. Before we can learn how to motivate ourselves in an ADHD-friendly way, we need to understand how our brains work and how we generally frame our world.

A Big Ball of Wibbly-Wobbly, Timey-Wimey

"I don't have an internal chronometer," I explained to friends years ago when we made plans to go to the beach. "I'm not sure why, but I don't sense the passing of time like other people seem to." This much I did know—I needed their help to let me know when to transition to the next activity, so I clued them in. "It will help if you give me a heads-up when we need to leave."

Even before I knew that I had ADHD, I understood that I did not have an accurate sense of time. I can't judge what time it is. And I can't tell you how many minutes or hours have passed since I began a task or activity or last checked the clock. My understanding of time fits much better with the Tenth Doctor from the British science fiction television program *Dr. Who*. He explains how time works: "People assume that time is a strict progression of cause to effect, but actually, from a nonlinear, nonsubjective viewpoint, it's more like a big ball of wibbly-wobbly, timey-wimey . . . stuff."[1] Time is, well, timey-wimey for me. I don't perceive it as a sequence but as a diffuse collection of events that are viscerally connected to the people, activities, and emotions involved in them.

If you have ADHD, this time issue is not in your imagination; time is more like a big ball of wibbly-wobbly, timey-wimey stuff for you too. Research shows what those with time blindness already know—individuals with ADHD have an impaired perception of time.[2] Researchers add that this is a substantial component of ADHD.

When it comes to practical approaches to time perception and its evaluation, we have difficulties with time estimation (knowing how long something will take) and discrimination activities (knowing what to do when). Although we have a general feeling that time passes, we feel disconnected from it, especially when completing tasks. This means we are poor judges of how long tasks take. We either overestimate the amount of time or underestimate it.

When Owen told me about a plumbing project he was going to do at home, he said the famous line that those of us with ADHD all say: "It really won't take that long." He thought it would take about thirty minutes.

I smiled and said, "Walk me through the steps you need to take to complete this project."

As he did, I could see the realization on his face that this project was going to take longer than he thought. He hadn't added the trip to the hardware store, clearing out the area beneath the sink, or the cleanup afterward.

As a general rule, I tell my clients to multiply their estimate of how much time something will take by three—unless it's unloading the dishwasher. "The dishwasher probably takes fifteen minutes to unload," I guessed one day, and I set a timer to see if I was right. I had been reading research about individuals with ADHD inaccurately judging time and wanted to test it for myself. I unloaded the dishwasher and looked at the timer on the stove. It still had ten minutes left! I was astonished to learn that it took under five minutes. I timed myself unloading the dishwasher for the next few weeks, and it was always under five minutes.

Like so many with ADHD, I dread the small duties around the house: unloading the dishwasher, hanging wet clothes on hangers to dry, and watering the tomato plants on the deck. They seem so tiresome. Because we dislike pesky little chores so much, we tend to overestimate how long they will take to complete.

This lack of time perception leads to a significant disadvantage in everyday life and often impedes performance at school or work. When one of my daughters with ADHD, Brooke, was in second grade, her teacher told her to watch the clock and leave for reading support at 10:15 on Wednesdays. Each Wednesday, she forgot to watch the clock and get to her special class, and as a consequence she lost her midday recess. Neither she nor her teacher had any idea that there was such a thing as time blindness, but both felt the effect of Brooke having it.

Expectations that students will have a basic awareness of time, like leaving the class at a certain point, are common in elementary and secondary schools. Teachers will ask students who are working on a task to provide an estimate of how many minutes remain until they complete it. This technique is meant to help students learn about time. But for those with ADHD, it creates an unfair assumption about their ability to understand time.

This time problem continues throughout their lives. Teachers, professors, and supervisors assume that those with ADHD have an intact perception of time. But they don't. And that lack can cause them great embarrassment. Although they can learn strategies for getting to places on time and calculating how much time tasks take, it will always be a strategy to employ, not an innate understanding.

Curious and Shiny

Here is an unconscious principle those with ADHD live by: *Fun things get my attention, and therefore fun tasks get done.* We are captivated by excitement and amusement, so our brains search the horizon for the interesting, the shiny, the curious, the remarkable, the exciting—and call it all "fun." This principle affects our levels of drive, our motivation, our happiness, and even our sense of well-being.

Though researchers think that several parts of the brain may be associated with the symptoms of ADHD, one area is particularly interesting when we are talking about the idea of fun. Right in the center of the brain is a part called the striatum. Known as the pleasure center of the brain, the striatum helps evaluate whether something is good and then allows us to experience joy and happiness. It is also able to learn to predict when rewards are coming.

Researchers wanted to find out if the striatum works differently in people who have ADHD. College students were shown a series of images as they lay in an MRI machine so that researchers could observe the active parts of the brain that lit up. The screen repeatedly showed the students a square shape and a diamond shape. After the diamond shape, sometimes a glass jar with coins appeared. The students were told that they would get some money on a gift card each time they saw the coins. But every time after the square shape was shown, a big X on the glass jar would appear, showing that they wouldn't get any money that time. As the college students saw different shapes and outcomes, researchers could see where their brains became more active.

Most people would start liking the diamond better than the square, right? They would begin to get excited when they saw a diamond because they knew what was coming next—a monetary reward. That seems logical, doesn't it? And that is how it played out for the students who did not have ADHD. The striatum lit up (became more active) when they saw the diamond shape and waited for the image of the coins to appear. It was anticipating the cue that "good things are coming soon!"

An interesting thing happened, however, when researchers viewed the scans of the students who had ADHD. Their striata didn't light up as much when they saw the diamond shape, even though it preceded the coin image indicating a reward would be coming soon. The striata in these brains didn't become active until the students actually saw the jar with coins. The striata of those with ADHD responded most when they actually received the reward, not while they were waiting for the reward.

The subjects in this study reacting to the *actual* rewards instead of the rewards coming in the future shows that the ADHD brain apparently lacks predictive abilities. Ugh. That's a problem for us as we attempt to begin a task. Without those brain signals in the striatum telling us that good things are coming and there's a reward just over the horizon, it's hard to begin or continue doing tasks and chores that are challenging or not so much fun. For example, you know that you need to complete your sales report for the month, but you just saw a new season of your favorite show dropped on Netflix. The show is exciting—much more exciting than your tedious report! So you decide to watch the show.

The results of the experiment suggest that, for those with ADHD, anticipation of a reward means nothing to their striatum. It takes the actual rewards or fun events to light up the striatum with excitement.[3] But for people who don't have ADHD, even before the actual rewards arrive, the striatum is buzzing with activity in response to signals that promise rewards will be coming.

The difference in how the striatum works between these two groups of people is important, because all of us, both humans and other animals, tend to repeat behaviors that are rewarding. If the striatum sends chemical signals that good things are coming, even tasks that aren't very enjoyable can be experienced as rewarding. Then a person is more likely to do the same thing again. For example, a neurotypical person works hard to finish a sales report, and his supervisor praises his timeliness and the thoroughness of his work. The next month, his striatum may already start becoming active during the time he is completing his worksheet, because his brain is expecting that same response from his boss. This helps sustain his focus and actions.

People with ADHD are more likely to repeat behaviors that bring actual and immediate rewards, like getting a good laugh from friends or getting fast food in a drive-through. The problem is that most of life doesn't work that way. We must tackle the difficult to get to the reward. Or we must accomplish the mundane to get to the fun. Learning to manage the rewards around us might help the striatum to become more active in ways that could help us accomplish what we want.

Our lack of time perception, our search for fun, and our inability to anticipate delayed gratification seriously interfere with knowing how and when to get things done. They are murderers of our motivation.

The Energy Drain

Our motivation is also affected by the amount of physical energy we *perceive* a task will require. We come to this conclusion by assigning each task a feeling, then through the lens of our hyperarousal, we gauge the difficulty of that task and how much energy it will use. Like with our estimations of time, we tend to overestimate or underestimate the amount of energy we will need.

Personally, how do I know how difficult a task will be ahead of time? How do I know how to prioritize? How do I gauge how much energy it will take? I check with my big emotions, and they tell me. And honestly, they aren't very accurate in their predictions. Folding laundry feels dull because I don't like it, so I think it will take a great deal of energy to complete. But I like vacuuming because of the neat lines that I can leave in the carpeting. It feels satisfying and doesn't seem to take any energy at all.

When I enjoy the tasks, I tend to consistently underestimate how much energy will be extracted from me. After working four consecutive twelve-hour days, I say to my husband, "Wow. I'm tired. How can I be this tired?" To him, it's logical why I am ready for bed at eight o'clock. For me, though, because I love my job and deeply enjoy working with clients, I forget how much energy it takes to coach and to accomplish the other tasks in my day.

Fatigue is one of the most common complaints that I hear from my clients when they talk about symptoms associated with ADHD, and usually they are referring to emotional fatigue. Why are we so exhausted? It is exhausting being us because we have feelings about every task that we do. Add the "big feels" to our other ADHD symptoms like anxiety, hyperactivity, and hyperfocus, and they take a toll on our energy level. We feel drained, like our batteries are constantly running on empty.

I have clients who have a low tolerance for the idea of losing energy. They worry that if they perform a certain task, they will lose too much energy and won't get it back. Tiffany is one of those people. She hates the feeling of the emotional overtiredness that accompanies her ADHD and avoids it by being extremely cautious about using any energy at all. When she does consider energy usage, she consistently overestimates the amount it will take to complete a chore. Thus, she is reluctant to begin her chores, saying she fears she will "get in too deep" and hyperfocus on the task. When I asked her what that meant, she explained, "What if I start cleaning up my kitchen and it takes all of my energy? I will have nothing left to give to my family." Tiffany forgets that, though cleaning up her kitchen after dinner will take some energy, she does not need to let the task consume all of it. She can learn to balance her energy intake with energy expenditures. Chapter 8 explores how to look at our metaphorical batteries and to keep them charged.

Emotional Intensity

Another way those of us with ADHD experience the world is by estimating how much emotional energy a task will require. Our delicate emotional brains are wired to detect even slight levels of emotional stimulation. So not only does each everyday activity have an emotion linked to it, but we also calculate the emotional intensity of it. We ask ourselves, "In terms of emotions, how interesting is this task to me?" Each task either is highly emotionally stimulating, creating convincing, strong emotions within us, or is on the other end of the spectrum with little emotional stimulation, providing punier, less interesting emotions.

This spectrum represents the volume control on our emotions. It doesn't matter if the feeling is positive or negative on this spectrum. The intensity of the feeling is what arouses us. When our ADHD brains get stimulated by the intensity of any emotion, our attention becomes focused. An example of positive, high emotional stimulus is going fishing with friends. We have a sense of (good) high emotional stimulation; we love the sunshine, the smell of the lake, and the time spent with good friends.

On the other hand, a high emotional stimulus can also occur when we have procrastinated and are hurrying to complete a project that is due in a few hours. We are stimulated, but instead of being excited and happy, we are rushed, angry, or even filled with self-loathing. Both situations are highly emotionally stimulating.

Some tasks, however, have little emotional stimulation. Emptying the dishwasher, doing homework, watching shows that we have already viewed on Netflix, or spending time on the internet may have little emotional stimulation.

We create these emotional labels from past experiences and other preconceived notions. What one person thinks is highly emotionally stimulating may not be what another thinks. For example, when my kids were teens, they watched *American Idol*. For them, the show was a low-emotional-stimulation activity. They relaxed and enjoyed it as they bantered with each other and chatted about the contestants and the judges' responses, forgetting about it within minutes of shutting off the television. My response was quite different. My heart rate became elevated. I felt stress and agitation, hating when the judges made rude comments or if there was drama on the set. Long after the show was over, I was still disturbed at what I had seen and experienced. This silly show was highly emotionally stimulating for me.

When I present the emotional intensity continuum to a large group, those without ADHD look puzzled, and someone will ask, "Are you saying that people with ADHD don't want to do something until there is a high emotional stimulus attached to it?"

The answer is yes. For those people, a high emotional stimulus feels like rocket fuel. In their daily life, something that has high emotion is much more likely to get done.

Perception of Interest

My idea of fun is not necessarily your idea of fun. For example, just the idea of playing golf makes me sad. Hitting a ball and following it around doesn't sound fun. (Driving the golf cart does, though.) But for some of my clients, playing golf is the epitome of fun.

When I present this concept of fun/not fun to large groups, I can tell who has ADHD and who doesn't just by their responses to the concept. Individuals with ADHD smile and nod vigorously as if they are saying, "Yes! Yes! That's how it works." They have an immediate reaction and know that they have strong preferences for FUN. They know that they are likely to build their whole days around what sparks their interest.

Non-ADHD individuals, on the other hand, nod slowly with a hint of confusion in their expressions. They are not driven by the need for fun and seem to respond moderately, "Sure, I like fun."

It's true that those without ADHD also distinguish between fun and not fun. The difference is that whether or not something is fun doesn't affect their motivation to act as significantly as it affects those with ADHD. Folks without ADHD are more likely to do not-fun activities just because they need to get them done.

Our fun/not-fun category differs from emotional intensity in that with intensity, the brain is not seeking enjoyment but rather responding to an emotional intensity we placed on the activity.

It's Really No Wonder

Reed thought about his frustrating situation for a minute. A father of a young daughter and with another baby on the way, Reed had been trying for months to get into a routine of managing the chores at his new house in the suburbs and performing well at his new job as a financial advisor. His wife was tired from the pregnancy, and he saw ways that he could help her. He knew what had to be done in the home and at work, but he couldn't find a way to motivate himself to do those things. None of the tasks were fun. And now he could see that combined with his poor concept of how time works and his feelings about tasks, he had created a stalemate in his head. "It's really no wonder why I can't motivate myself," he said.

Reed had the same problem that most of us with ADHD have—we struggle with how and where to begin. Task initiation includes overcoming procrastination and getting started on tasks even if we don't want to do them. Many of us with ADHD don't realize that we naturally (and unconsciously) ask ourselves two questions as we consider a task: Will it be fun? How emotionally interesting is this for me?

To help my clients like Reed understand time and tasks through an ADHD lens, I created the Solve-It Grid. This grid helps us identify how we are categorizing a particular activity so we can frame or reframe it and then take charge of how we respond. After we realize how we think and feel about a task, we can use specific strategies to manage our efforts. When we start with the Solve-It Grid, we apply our natural (ADHD) way of understanding time and tasks. This grid will help us discover what is getting in the way of us beginning and completing a job.

The Solve-It Grid

The Solve-It Grid, which we will discuss in detail in the next chapter, is based on two ADHD inclinations:

- *Perception of interest.* This is the degree to which a person with ADHD considers how fun an activity will be when deciding how to accomplish a task.
- *Emotional intensity.* This is the degree to which a person with ADHD calculates how much emotional energy a task will take.

In the next chapter, we will assemble two continuums of perception of interest and emotional intensity to create the four quadrants of the Solve-It Grid. Learning how to use this grid can help you manage your emotions and behavior. The Solve-It Grid can help you with engage with a task instead of avoiding it, tolerate emotional discomfort instead of becoming overwhelmed, and switch modes of working instead of failing to implement a plan.

8

Living on the Grid

"I'm on 10 percent power," I warned my husband while we talked over the phone. My old iPhone had a weak battery. Because it took such a long time to charge and drained faster than I wanted it to, I was usually aware of the percentage that I had left. I had to be very careful about how I used my battery throughout the day. I had cords and chargers located everywhere: tucked in my purse, in my car, at my office, and, of course, at home, just in case I needed to find a power source quickly.

After charging my phone all night, I checked the weather before getting out of bed. *How many layers will I need to wear on this winter day?* I wondered. That knowledge cost me—I was already down to 93 percent of my battery life. I went to work, and by 10:00 a.m., I was down to 65 percent. At lunch, I was at 53 percent. Checking my calendar via the web cost 3 percent. If I needed to stop by the grocery store, I'd be down to 30 percent or less by the time I got home.

Battery Awareness

We all have our own internal limited battery energy. But those with ADHD find that their battery—like the one in my old cell phone—is prone to becoming more quickly and easily depleted from activities that others may not find taxing at all. Duties that I find tedious, like answering emails, invoicing clients, going grocery shopping, and returning phone calls, can feel as though they drain at least 50 percent of my daily battery. For some people, those activities might consume only 5 percent of their daily battery allotment. When I manage my energy and recharge at frequent intervals, my battery is less likely to die (lose all power) and I am more productive throughout my day.

Everyone has a different set of activities that drain them. For some, meeting a friend for coffee can be enriching but also exhausting. For others, spending a great deal of time alone reduces their battery percentage. Planning a complicated meeting can energize some and deplete others. Knowing what charges our batteries and what depletes them is vital for our physical and mental health. If we don't pay attention to the amount of energy we lose, our batteries die, and we feel discouraged, sad, even dysphoric.

As I discussed in the previous chapter, those of us with ADHD have difficulty seeing and managing energy expenditure. So we are especially in need of a way to frame our tasks that will help us become energy efficient. I'm hoping that you will find that the Solve-It Grid will get you started in this direction.

We discussed in the last chapter how we instinctively classify activities as fun or not fun and how we use high-intensity emotions or low-intensity emotions to accomplish those activities. The Solve-It Grid[1] will help us identify how we are categorizing a particular activity and to take charge of how we respond. After realizing how we think and feel about a task, we can use specific strategies to manage our batteries—our energy and efforts.

The Solve-It Grid

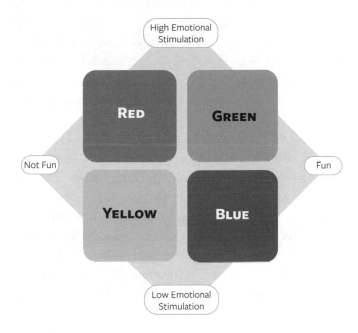

The Red Quadrant

The Red Quadrant is where we subconsciously place tasks and activities that aren't fun for us but are highly emotionally stimulating. You may wonder, *How can something be not fun and yet get my emotional attention and energize me?* If you recall from chapter 6, we use malicious emotional tricks like anxiety or anger to help us complete a job. When we tackle an activity in this quadrant, we work ourselves into a heightened emotional state in order to complete the task. For example, procrastination—delaying a job until it requires immediate attention—is a way of dealing with a task in the Red Quadrant. When we've procrastinated too long, we get anxious and feel like we now need to respond quickly, causing an adrenaline rush. At first, Red feels energizing because of that initial rush, but ultimately, operating for too long in this quadrant, no matter what emotion is used, is exhausting. However, it can also be addictive because our frantic feelings are connected to a sense of achievement. It's not long before we learn to rely on those frenzied actions to be productive. We find we can motivate ourselves to get things done by pushing them off until the last minute, but we drain our batteries in the process.

Mark discovered that he was addicted to Red tasks. He said that he felt more "effective and alive" when he waited to start a report until an hour before it was due, didn't fill his gas tank until it was nearly empty, or completed urgent matters at his job. He over-loaded his calendar, procrastinated, and then pushed himself to deliver at the last minute. Even his hobbies reflected his obsession with Red—he loved skydiving, motorcycle racing, and boxing. "I like speed," he boasted at our first meeting. "It's how I like to get things done. Last year, I increased my sales by 15 percent. Success means never slowing down."

It sounds as though Mark is succeeding well in his job, but clearly there's an issue, because his supervisor recommended that he make an appointment with me. Although Mark couldn't see it, others were affected by his behavior. And contrary to what he believes, Mark can't thrive while living mostly in the Red Quadrant. He will burn out, and his battery will take a long time to recharge.

Spending time in the Red Quadrant isn't wrong, but spending too much time there has severe effects on our minds and bodies, leaving us feeling tired and possibly resulting in burnout. At the end of this book, I've included a helpful tool titled "Your Life on the Grid" to help you assess where you are and how to navigate moving between the colors on the grid. For the moment, let's just look at things in the Red Quadrant. If you can, go ahead and write your answers in the space provided.

My tasks that are usually in the Red Quadrant:

_____

_____

What it is about these tasks that make them Red for me:

_____

_____

The Yellow Quadrant

A high school senior, Nora, looked at the Solve-It Grid that I had drawn on a small whiteboard in my office. "Which quadrant do you avoid the most?" I asked her.

Like most clients who see this grid for the first time, she pointed to the Yellow Quadrant. It contains tasks and activities that aren't fun and are not emotionally stimulating.

"Why is this the one that you avoid?" I asked.

Without hesitation, she said, "This quadrant is boring and repetitive. Nothing is interesting here." Things in the Yellow Quadrant are tasks like homework, housework, logging sales calls, and paying bills. Doing these things isn't difficult, but because they don't ignite or hold our interest, we put off doing them. Most of my clients see items in this quadrant as a nuisance, so they neglect, avoid, or wish them away.

"Does Red or Yellow drain your battery faster?" I asked Nora.

This time she needed to think. "Well, Red actually drains my battery faster, but Yellow feels like it totally drains my battery." She looked at me. "I hate Yellow and try not to do it. But Yellow probably doesn't drain my battery like I think, does it?" The very thought of doing Yellow tasks does seem draining, but as Nora discovered, they do not drain our energy rapidly.

Nora tried an experiment. Instead of putting off her AP literature class reading until the last minute and making it a Red task, Nora decided to read fifteen pages as a Yellow Quadrant task. She planned what she would read and set a timer for twenty minutes. "I didn't finish all of the reading, but I made a lot of progress. And it wasn't as difficult as I thought it would be. Setting a timer helped me realize that Yellow wasn't going to last forever." Nora found a trick to approach Yellow tasks and accomplish them without draining her battery.

It is easy to misjudge the amount of energy Yellow tasks consume. We mistakenly think that spending time in the Yellow Quadrant will deplete more energy than time spent in Red. However, the truth is that the Yellow Quadrant, although containing activities that are not interesting and not fun, only gradually depletes our batteries.

My tasks that are usually in the Yellow Quadrant:

_____

_____

What it is about these tasks that make them Yellow for me:

_____

_____

The Blue Quadrant

The Blue Quadrant is where we participate in fun, low-effort activities. Because they don't take a lot of emotional effort, they also don't bring much emotional stimulation. Time spent in Blue is useful because it gives our busy brains time to relax and allows for calm entertainment. Activities in Blue may consist of playing games on our phone, lying in a hammock, and taking a bath. Operating within the Blue Quadrant slowly recharges our batteries.

The problem with this quadrant is that it is challenging for those of us with ADHD to get the balance right. Too little Blue makes us anxious and desiring play and rest, while too much Blue makes us sluggish and even more resistant to accomplishing tasks. The Blue Quadrant is like food. We need it to survive, but we need healthy food and not too much of it. When we get the beneficial types of Blue in a healthy amount, our batteries are charged. When we snack or gorge on unhealthy Blue, our batteries are slower to replenish.

What is a healthy Blue for you? It all depends. For example, scrolling through Twitter for a few minutes may be relaxing for you. That is probably a healthy Blue for you and will slowly recharge your battery. On the other hand, perhaps scanning posts causes you to feel envious, anxious, or angry. That is not a healthy Blue and won't charge your battery well. You are probably wasting more energy and quickly draining your battery. Without realizing it, you have left the ease of Blue and moved to Red.

For clients like twenty-nine-year-old Liam, the Blue Quadrant was a seemingly safe place to go when he didn't want to do what he needed to do. But it was actually a seductive trap. Liam loved to meet his friends online and play video games after work. "It's so relaxing and helps me forget about my day at work," he said.

When we want to distract ourselves from tasks in the Yellow and Red Quadrants, we instinctively want to go to Blue. But we can get stuck there. We tell ourselves that we will check Instagram for "just a moment," and two hours of clicking go by. Sometimes the Blue Quadrant is like the molasses swamp from Candy Land, and we find ourselves unable to get out of the sticky mess of binge-watching a Netflix show. This "just one more" approach to life keeps us stuck in Blue. For Liam, the Blue low-key fun became problematic because he spent too much time in this quadrant and not enough in varying activities.

My tasks that are usually in the Blue Quadrant:

_____

_____

What it is about these tasks that make them Blue for me:

_____

_____

The Green Quadrant

The Green Quadrant is our very happy place. It includes activities that are fun *and* emotionally stimulating. Green gives us space to build relationships, reflect on personal growth, be creative, and enjoy our lives. It often refocuses our purposes and goals, reminding us what is truly important. In this way, Green has a transformative effect. Green activities can include spending time with family and friends, going for a walk on a beautiful day, seeing beautiful artwork, or watching the sunset. We feel refreshed, more hopeful, and closer to our authentic selves.

One of my favorite Green activities is having a meal with our whole family. I find myself relishing moments of our time together, especially after dinner, when the once carefully set table is messy, the dirty dishes and cloth napkins are piled on the corner, and my adult children continue their banter and laughter. There is a warm and lively atmosphere in our small dining room. My husband and I exchange looks; we know that this is a good moment. For days after a family meal, I will still feel the glow of those moments. Even though it took work—cleaning the house, planning and making the dinner—the family dinner recharged my battery. When I spend time in Green, I am reminded of what I value.

It is natural for us to want to spend time in the Green Quadrant, but many of us don't. Many of my clients have a deficit of Green in their lives. They feel as if they don't deserve it or don't want to take the time to invest in it. In a workshop where I presented the Solve-It Grid, one participant said, "I punish myself all the time by not allowing Green time into my day." In a different workshop, another person said, "Is it really okay for me to enjoy Green? I always feel guilty when I do something really fun. I think I should be doing something more productive." These participants were missing out on this quadrant because they mistakenly believed that they didn't merit it.

Other clients underestimate the benefit of Green and think it will require too much of their energy. They don't want the hassle of deciding which Green activity to do, getting out of their chair or house, and actually finding the motivation to do it. They often settle for lower emotional activities in Blue because they feel like they will recharge faster.

Blue and Green both recharge a person's battery—but at very different rates. The Green Quadrant, because it is fun and emotionally interesting, is the fastest way to restore a flagging emotional-energy battery. After Green experiences, a person may feel refreshed, more creative, or more centered. Blue activities, if not overly used, can recharge the battery but at a slower rate. If indulged too long, Blue will actually deplete the battery rather than recharge it.

My tasks that are usually in the Green Quadrant:

_____

_____

What it is about these tasks that make them Green for me:

_____

_____

117

Practice Awareness

One of the most important things that you can do to manage your ADHD is to manage your energy expenditure. Like I did with my aging cell phone, keeping track of your emotional-battery levels will help you become more proficient in using your time and energy wisely. A way to increase your awareness of those levels is by assessing how different activities affect your energy. As you find yourself in an activity, ask:

1. Is this task fun or not fun?
2. How emotionally stimulating is this activity?
3. How is my energy increasing or decreasing?
4. In which color quadrant is this task or activity located?

Having trouble? Move the job or activity around the grid until you find its accurate placement.

Delve deeper to discover which aspects of an activity cause it to be located in a particular quadrant. Is there a way that you might be able to shape this task differently or shift it into a healthier, energy-sustaining quadrant?

Thinking through Your Tasks

Now that you understand the basics of the Solve-It Grid and have some awareness of which tasks go where, you can start using it to become more energy efficient.

Let's say you just discovered that the task you need to accomplish is in the Yellow Quadrant. Oof. You don't like that quadrant. Take a breath and acknowledge the discomfort of it. Besides your task being an undesirable Yellow, what else do you dread about it? Erin, a dental hygienist, told me that she hates completing her patient documentation because she's worried that she will mess it up. Her fear of making a mistake adds to the grief of doing an already boring Yellow task.

Use the questions in the "Your Life on the Grid" appendix to create a how-to list to help you approach your task. This list breaks down the task into simple and specific steps. Yes, it takes time. Yes, each step may seem too obvious to write down. But remember that for those of us with ADHD, sequencing tasks is difficult, and the difficulty adds to our mental clutter. Making a set of directions for task completion helps create order from the chaos.

Commit to at least fifteen minutes of working on this activity. Maren liked Nora's idea of setting a timer. But she took it a step further. "I bought a timer shaped like a little pink pig. I set it for twenty or thirty minutes and place it on my desk so its little pink snout will point at me when the time is up." Maren pulled the pig from her bag for a show-and-tell moment, placing it on her palm. "This helps me to visually stay on task. I can watch his little head turning slowly and know that yes, time is passing, and yes, very soon it's going to ring. He also helps me auditorily. When I'm tempted to go to a 'quick' email or look at the news headlines, the ticking reminds me that I'm on task . . . but when the bell rings, I will have ten minutes to do whatever I want."

At the end of your allotted minutes, have you hit a sense of flow? If yes, keep going! If not, take a quick break, take a deep, slow breath, and ask yourself, "What is getting in the way of completing this task?"

- Is it an emotional reason (e.g., *I just hate this work so much, I don't want to do it*)?

- Is it a technical reason (e.g., *I don't have the information I need*)?

- Is it a cognitive reason (e.g., *I don't understand how to complete this*)?

Address what is hindering your progress. If it is an emotional reason, take a break from it. Set your timer for another twenty minutes and return to the work after the break. Most likely your frustration will have dissipated. If the hindrance is a technical reason, rewrite your how-to list to include what you need to do in order to finish the task. If it is a cognitive reason, return to your how-to list and revise it to include learning what you will need to know in order to finish the task.

Ask yourself:

1. Why is this task in this quadrant?
2. How will I begin? (Be very specific.)
3. When will I do this? (Set a specific time to begin and end.)
4. Where will I do this activity?
5. What might be emotionally distracting to me while I work? How will I manage that?
6. How will I guard myself against the malicious motivators?

Becoming Energy Efficient

How do you get things done? Writing detailed goals or long to-do lists doesn't make sense. Using malicious motivation is cruel to yourself. Instead, take time to acknowledge how you feel about a task. Do you like it or hate it? Do you have strong emotions about it or little emotional interest? Find the job's location on the grid. Clarifying your thoughts is essential to how you approach the task. Make a plan for accomplishing the mission by creating your how-to list.

Predictable Patterns

For those of us with ADHD, mindfully managing our battery usage helps us accomplish more tasks and feel better about ourselves. Unfortunately, though, we get stuck in behavior patterns that keep us from using our resources well. Our unconscious patterns feel comfortable to us, so we don't realize how damaging they are to our energy levels, productivity, and relationships. We can use the Solve-It Grid to help evaluate our mistaken beliefs, create better habits, and improve our performance. When we examine our behavior in the different quadrants, we learn what ensnares our thinking.

As you read through the following patterns, identify which patterns you use.

The Need-for-Speed Pattern

Operating in the Red Quadrant is like pushing the panic button in your body each time you need to complete a task. When you use the Need-for-Speed pattern, you tend to create tension and pressures in your life—on either a conscious or an unconscious level. Responding to a self-manufactured crisis triggers the body's stress response. When you rely on this pattern, you get a rush that comes with excitement. You might say that you work best under stressful circumstances. Though that may be true, it comes at a high cost. This pattern places incredible stress on your body, especially the nervous system. If you use the Need-for-Speed pattern, you are writing checks that your body eventually won't be able to cash.

Remember Mark? He was the go-getter in the previous chapter who preferred to get things done in the Red Quadrant. He loved life in the Red and was exhilarated by hitting life hard and fast. He was rewarded for this addiction for a while because his coworkers saw him as a strong leader. Over time, though, his coworkers and his supervisor grew tired of his constant "push to excellence." Now, after two decades of living at this breakneck speed, Mark realizes there are costs. At a recent doctor visit, he was surprised to learn that even though he was in great shape, he showed signs that his body was in constant stress. "I couldn't believe what I was hearing," Mark said in his quick-paced staccato. "I train so hard." His doctor strongly advised him to find ways to slow down. Mark needed to address his Need-for-Speed pattern before the consequences became severe.

See how you score in the Need-for-Speed pattern. Give yourself 1 point for each yes answer:

1. Do you always seem to have a crisis going in your life (real or overblown)?
2. Does getting angry help you work better?
3. Are you always rushing, with a packed schedule?
4. Would others say that you often have dramatic conflicts or outbursts of intense emotion?
5. Do you feel guilty if you use your spare time to relax?
6. Do you need to win to derive enjoyment from games and sports?

7. Do you generally move, walk, and eat rapidly?

8. Are your physical movements hurried?

9. Do you thrive or feel exhilarated under pressure?

10. Do you (or others) consider yourself a high achiever?

If you scored above 7, you probably have an issue with this pattern and will want to address it.

I tend to use the Need-for-Speed pattern to manage my life. I feel invigorated when my schedule is packed and I need to be "on." Throughout each day, I need to remind myself to slow down. Here are some strategies that I use to change this pattern.

1. *Addressing False Beliefs.* Learn to listen for the false beliefs that are keeping you overcommitted. False beliefs are created over many years, and people cement these beliefs without questioning their validity. Sometimes the false belief in the Need-for-Speed pattern is, "If I am able to complete a lot of things in one day, it must mean I've done a good job and therefore I'm a good enough person."

The problem with this thinking is that I may accomplish a lot but not prioritize the most important tasks. With the more-is-better thinking, I'm likely to waste time on low-impact, easy-to-complete tasks just to feel good about what I've accomplished rather than doing what truly needed to be done.

Another false belief I often see connected with this pattern is when someone incorrectly associates self-worth with checking things off a to-do list. The belief that "I am a worthy human being only when I accomplish things" is a dangerous pattern and will harm your emotional health.

There are many false beliefs that can be tied to this pattern. What is your false belief that keeps you in the Need-for-Speed pattern?

2. *Morning Practice.* Take fifteen minutes first thing in the morning to breathe and pray.

Yes, I need to be reminded to breathe. When I slow my breathing down, it takes me out of the fight-or-flight feeling. My brain can focus on God and his promised presence throughout my day. As I make my daily list, I include Yellow Quadrant tasks and Blue Quadrant activities.

3. *Midday Practice.* Try setting a midday alarm for a system check.

When I was first learning to manage the Need-for-Speed pattern, I stopped when the alarm went off and ran through a few questions. Was my posture relaxed or tense? Did I need food, water, or to use the bathroom? Did I need to take a brief walk around the house to stretch my muscles? I was initially surprised at check-in time at how tense my neck and jaw were and how I had forgotten to tend to my basic physical needs.

4. *Evening Practice.* Spend ten minutes each evening reviewing your day.

Very intentionally, I appreciate what I accomplished during the day. I used to shame myself for not completing enough and had to teach myself this different approach. Now, although I haven't completed everything on my list (it is longer than can be completed by anyone in a day), I am pleased with my work. Then I make notes to myself about what I would like to achieve tomorrow.

The Playing-with-Fire Pattern

The Playing-with-Fire pattern begins when an uninteresting task is resting in the Yellow Quadrant and you wait until it creeps toward Red.

Using this approach—avoiding your mundane task in Yellow until it turns into a Red emergency—is like setting a tiny campfire in a dry, wooded area. You don't think much about managing the campfire because it's so small. It grows a bit, but still you do nothing. Suddenly, the fire begins to engulf the surrounding area—and now you act. But because you waited too long, the small campfire has grown into a forest fire, too big for you to manage. As a result, there will be damage and casualties.

Students and workers who wait until the last minute to begin a project and then must scramble to get it done are playing with this campfire. They use their increasing anxiety to meet their deadline as adrenaline and other intensely focused neurochemicals kick in to put out the forest fire.

Gia used this pattern much of the time to complete work for her job and graduate school. "I planned to do it ahead of time, but I just didn't seem to know when or how to start until it was too late," she said. "Then, after I finished the project, I felt sad. I mean, super sad. Like I let myself down. I would be mad at myself for not getting it done earlier."

Those who rely on the Playing-with-Fire pattern frequently talk about the shame they feel after completing the task they'd postponed. This pattern differs from the Need-for-Speed approach because those who use it don't get to enjoy the Red Quadrant's thrill. Like Gia, most people who use this pattern have unmet expectations about their performance and ability to complete a Yellow task.

Some people who use this pattern will also deny themselves Green Quadrant time because they believe they haven't earned it. When I asked Gia why she refused herself Green Quadrant activities that were fun and energizing, she pointed to tasks in the Red and Yellow Quadrants, saying, "This is what being a grown-up looks like. And I'll never get all of this stuff done." This denial of pleasure is a way of punishing themselves for not being good at Yellow tasks, so they place all their energy in only the Red and Yellow Quadrants.

See how you score on the Playing-with-Fire pattern. Give yourself 1 point for each yes answer:

1. Do you often find yourself rushing to complete important tasks that you had intended to do days before?
2. Do you delay simple tasks that require little more than sitting down and doing them?

3. Do you often waste time doing other things when you are trying to prepare for a deadline?

4. Are you constantly saying, "I'll do it tomorrow"?

5. Do you waste a lot of time on trivial matters before getting to a decision?

6. Even after you make a decision, do you usually delay acting on it?

7. Do you find yourself constantly running out of time?

8. Is your fear of making mistakes stopping you from getting started?

9. Do you often make excuses for not doing your best work?

10. Do you wish you could take a break and have some relaxing fun without guilt?

If you scored above 6, you will want to examine your pattern with deadlines. As with each of the patterns, there is always a cost. If you utilize this pattern, is the cost that you produce less-than-professional work? Is it the unnecessary depletion of your energy? Is emotional exhaustion the price you pay? Don't despair! There is hope for you. You *can* do things differently.

If you use this pattern, there is a battle waging in your brain. You know what you should do, but you don't do it. Avoidance is usually at the center of this pattern. Unusual coping mechanisms like procrastination, passive-aggressiveness, and rumination sneak in either consciously or unconsciously as you avoid tackling a tough issue or facing uncomfortable thoughts and feelings. Here are some strategies that my clients use to change this pattern.

1. *Addressing False Beliefs.* Confront your false beliefs that keep you working in this pattern. One limiting belief might be "I work well under pressure." I know that it feels like you do, but you don't. You are using your anxious thoughts to bolster yourself. This is exhausting.

Another false belief associated with this pattern is the belief that you should only focus on getting Yellow tasks done. Although you frequently slip into Blue Quadrant activities, you scold yourself for that and push back to Yellow and then Red. The loop that you create by sliding into Blue and forcing yourself back to Yellow and Red is exhausting. You need to create more balance in your approach to managing the grid.

2. *Morning Practice.* Schedule fifteen minutes each morning to view your Yellow tasks. (I suggest you limit your Yellow tasks to only three to five items.) What makes something a Yellow task? Is there a task that seems boring or otherwise yucky? Ask yourself why you are tempted to avoid that task on your list.

Break the ugly Yellow task into small, how-to steps. I often hear my clients say when talking about Yellow tasks, "I don't even know where to start." This is because very often, the job that they are procrastinating on feels too big or too vague. Take the time to write the steps out, no matter how small they seem. This simple practice will help you see how to complete the task.

Make an agreement with yourself that you will work on the Yellow item for twenty minutes. If after that time you haven't gotten into the flow of it, then move to a different task.

3. *Midday Practice.* Review your Yellow list. How many of the items on your list could move to the Red Quadrant if you delay them? (Gulp. I just thought of a few on my list that I have conveniently let burn.) How can you address these tasks now instead of waiting for the feeling of urgency?

4. *Evening Practice.* How well did you stay out of the Red Quadrant today? Were you able to think more clearly when you weren't in that quadrant? What key behaviors worked for you through Yellow Quadrant tasks? Were you more aware of the times when you were slipping into Blue Quadrant activities? What did you do to refocus your efforts?

Although you may not have finished everything on your list, appreciate what you did accomplish. It was a long list.

The Red, Blue, and Back Again Pattern

In this energy pattern, we move from the Red Quadrant to the Blue and then back to Red. Tasks in the Red Quadrant seem to hold us in a frantic, frenzied state. We tell ourselves that we are the most productive there, and we work there for as long as we can. And then we flop to Blue because we are tired, depleted, and sometimes even sad. Then we muster our anxiety, anger, or whatever strong emotion we need to spur us back to Red.

I used this pattern for years—and sometimes am tempted to return to it. For me, it looks like this. I work diligently all week, long hours, with no margins for Blue or Green. Then on Friday evening, I sink into my sofa, mumble something about leaving it all on the field this week, and slip into a catatonic state. I am in for serious veg time. Then Monday morning, I am scared out of bed by all that I need to do and go right back into the Red Quadrant. The problem with this approach to life is that the all-or-nothing pattern robs you of emotional balance and leaves you missing out on the sweet moments of life.

There was a time in my life when I was teaching college full-time, writing a dissertation, and taking courses, and I had three children, ages three months, seven years, and nine years. I had so much to do—and it felt like everything depended on me. One day, I sat to watch a television show with my kids as the baby slept on my chest. It was the first time I had stopped all day. I could feel my breath matching the slow breathing of my sleeping infant. My eyes closed as my chin rested on her sweet-smelling head. I was starting to drift off when I heard my always-observant seven-year-old note in a loud whisper, "Have you ever noticed that Mom is like a doll? If she tips over, her eyes shut."

This pattern is different from the Need-for-Speed pattern, which is for adrenaline junkies who engage in Red effectively all day and rest just enough to continue in Red the next day. The Red, Blue, and Back Again pattern has days or weeks in the productive Red

Quadrant followed by days or weeks in unproductive Blue. The telltale sign of this pattern is intense behavior one minute and a blithe attitude the next.

See how you score on the Red, Blue, and Back Again pattern. Give yourself 1 point for each yes answer:

1. Are you very competitive and self-critical, only to suddenly flip and become complacent?
2. Do you strive relentlessly toward goals without feeling a sense of joy in your efforts or accomplishments?
3. Do you find at times that you know you should be doing something productive but are too fatigued mentally or physically to do anything at all, only to press yourself into hyper-action a day or two later?
4. Do you get wound up quickly and overreact sometimes, but other times you just don't care?
5. Do you experience a driving, persistent sense of urgency to complete tasks?
6. Do you find yourself flipping between being incredibly impatient some days and very tolerant on others?
7. Do you look like you have two speeds: on and off?
8. Do you sometimes forget to enjoy the journey?
9. When you realize that you forgot to enjoy the journey, does that make you feel sad or down?
10. Although you know you should take more time to relax, do you find that idea unappealing?
11. Do you stop and rest only when your body tells you that you must (through sickness, fatigue, etc.)?

If you scored above 7, you will want to think about how you can balance your energy use. As with the Playing-with-Fire pattern, if you utilize this pattern, is the cost less-than-professional work?

Is it a complete depletion of your energy? Is the price you pay the emotional exhaustion you feel? Fortunately, people who use this pattern are natural problem solvers. Here are some strategies to help you address the challenges of this pattern.

1. *Addressing False Beliefs.* If you use this pattern, you are very likely to believe that you can't slow down because there is so much to do and you are already behind. Life will always feel big and busy, so remember to respect the necessity for balance in your life. Appreciate the refreshment given to you by Green Quadrant activities. Learn how Yellow Quadrant activities can be easier on you and your energy than Red ones.

2. *Morning Practice.* As you decide what to include in your day, make sure that items from the Yellow, Green, and Blue Quadrants are represented on your list. Think about why it is important to have all these quadrants represented throughout your day.

3. *Midday Practice.* If you use this pattern, you likely have a never-ending to-do list. Check in on the list you made that morning. Have you added other colors besides Red and Yellow? If not, how can you add a few minutes of another quadrant now?

4. *Evening Practice.* End your workday at a set time. Reflect on your relationships. Your having only two speeds can be difficult for those who live and work with you. Your intense activity one day and exhaustion the next may confuse or even drain others. Make a list of the relationships that are important to you and then schedule Green time with those people.

The Nothin'-but-Blue Pattern

TJ had a Nothin'-but-Blue pattern. He looks like an easygoing person who just wants to enjoy his life. I first met TJ when he was twenty-three and living at his parents' home. Although he was smart, he was convinced that neither college nor training school would be a good fit for him. He spent his days hanging out with his band, playing first-person-shooter video games, planning campaigns for Dungeons and Dragons, and working part-time delivering pizzas. "I'm not sure that I know what I want to do," he explained, "so I don't do anything." His smile was sweetly disarming as he talked. He carefully avoided tasks that weren't fun and might involve any negative emotions.

Although it is common for people to seek to avoid at least some anxiety-provoking situations, TJ had become an expert at it, entrenched in his choice to avoid Red and Yellow Quadrant tasks. "It probably started in high school," he told me. "I hated school so much that I started skipping classes." TJ is more of an avoider than a procrastinator. His urge to escape situations that were uncomfortable provided relief that felt good and reinforced the Nothin'-but-Blue pattern.

This pattern differs from plain old procrastination because the person who uses it has no intention of engaging in an undesirable task. They steer clear of getting tangled up in any anxiety that Yellow or Red Quadrant activities may cause and find distractions and shelter in Blue. Like TJ, they occupy themselves with entertainment or some sort of busywork. Life often feels too complicated and too meticulous for them, and Blue is a cozy place to stay for a while.

See how you score on the Nothin'-but-Blue pattern. Give yourself 1 point for each yes answer:

1. I question why tasks have to be so difficult all the time.
2. I find myself waiting for inspiration before starting important tasks, and while I wait I might as well _____ [insert Blue activity].
3. I know what I have to do, but frequently I find I am spending my time doing something else that is more enjoyable.
4. When tired, I really just want to veg out rather than tackle any of the difficult tasks I face.
5. I see how workaholics don't enjoy life—so I refuse to be one.

131

6. If I forgo the small things that make me happy, then I will become a boring, lifeless drone.

7. Even if I tried to _____ [insert task], I wouldn't know where to start.

8. I often imagine people criticizing my work before I even complete it.

9. Social situations can be very uncomfortable for me, and I fear being rejected or criticized.

10. I am reluctant to take risks or engage in new activities that may prove embarrassing.

If you scored above 6, you will want to examine your pattern of hiding from the stress of performing tasks. As with each of the patterns, there is a cost to hanging out in Nothin'-but-Blue. If you have this pattern, is the cost that you are not following your dreams? Is it a dissatisfaction with your life? Do you pay the price by not having close relationships?

When work is boring or unpleasant, there's too much to do, or it's too hard to figure out where to start, you might be tempted to kick back in the Nothin'-but-Blue pattern. Here are some strategies to consider that may help you step out of this pattern.

1. *Addressing False Beliefs.* There are three common false beliefs that I see when individuals use this pattern.

a. You are likely concerned about conserving all your energy. Examine your false belief of fearing that any tasks in Yellow, Red, or even Green may require an abundance of energy.

b. Another false belief is that if you can't do it perfectly, you won't even take the risk. Examine how you have endorsed perfectionism in your life, and expose it for the lie that it is—no one does anything perfectly.

c. Hidden deep within this pattern is the false belief that if you perform flawlessly, you will gain people's acceptance and love. The fear of letting someone down by failing at a task is so great that you choose not to do anything.

2. *Morning Practice.* Face the Blue. What Blue Quadrant distractions may get in your way today? What activity drags you into the Nothin'-but-Blue pattern? Are you addicted to it? Can you easily stop the activity? For example, if it is a game on your phone or computer, try going twenty-four hours without engaging in it.

3. *Midday Practice.* Make a goal of completing three tasks in the Yellow Quadrant today. You can do more than you think when your energy is low. Try setting a timer for twenty minutes to begin a Yellow task. Energy, stress, motivation, and mood often improve if you tackle things step-by-step rather than resting in a Blue activity.

Try the Yellow-Blue game: work for thirty minutes, then take a ten-minute Blue break. The critical detail here is to set a timer. Many of my clients have used this with a lot of success. TJ told me, "I accidentally continued in a Yellow task because I really got into it."

4. *Evening Practice.* When your three Yellow Quadrant tasks are completed, treat yourself to a longer, relaxing Blue Quadrant activity. Or, better yet, do a Green Quadrant activity that will nourish your energy level.

One of the ways that we can manage our ADHD is to watch for what patterns we are using and to address them the best we can. This is difficult work because it takes a concerted effort to expose our false beliefs and practice better habits. While the Solve-It Grid can't actually do our laundry or pay our bills, it can help us balance those tasks in a clear picture of how we spend our time and energy.

10

Climbing the Ladder

Cultivating Emotional Health

It was my busiest time of the year. Each minute of my day, it seemed, was spoken for. I reminded myself that this feeling of drinking from a fire hose would not last much longer. After that, I could return to a more normal, balanced life. "If I am going to live in the Red Quadrant for a while," I reflected, "then I need to remain healthy." I took the precautions that would help me keep up with the busy pace: eating well, sleeping at least eight hours, and carefully planning each day.

Knowing that I have ADHD and being well versed in all its tricks and nuances, I tried to compensate by thoughtfully regulating my behavior. When I woke in the morning, I rehearsed the day, reviewing each appointment and task on my calendar. I believed that if I focused on particular executive functions—task initiation, planning, time management, and organization—then I would be able to manage this busy time successfully.

I was wrong. Although those executive function areas are indeed crucial to my success, there were others I was not accounting for: emotional control, flexibility, and self-monitoring. I had thought I was using all my executive functions, but I wasn't. Instead, I was resorting to reliance on my limbic system—a common ADHD error.

I woke one morning and prepared for what I thought was my thoroughly planned day. Just a few moments before my first session was to begin, my friend Cameron Gott, a fellow ADHD coach, texted me, "Sent the Zoom invite."

I had no idea what he was talking about. And then my stomach tightened. *Oh no!* He and I were supposed to meet to finalize our joint presentation for an upcoming conference. My thoughts raced. I had totally forgotten about this meeting. *Wait—wasn't I going to ask him if we could move it to Friday? Did I ever send that text? How did I miss this? He's counting on me. He must think I'm an idiot.* My thoughts spiraled. I had screwed up again! What a loser! If I couldn't even run my own life, how could I help anyone else with their ADHD?

You'll remember from previous chapters that those with ADHD have unreliable access to their PFC and compensate for it by overusing the limbic systems that govern emotion and memory. Tom Brown, a Yale-trained clinical psychologist who specializes in assessment and treatment of ADHD, reminds us, "Sometimes the working memory impairments of ADHD [in the PFC] allow a momentary emotion to become too strong, flooding the brain with one intense emotion."[1] In other words, when our PFCs are not working effectively or are overtaxed, our limbic systems go on high alert, scanning the horizon for danger. Our brains fail to distinguish between true dangerous threats and more minor annoyances.

You have probably noticed that some days you feel like you can master your ADHD symptoms—you are cognizant, in control, and aware—while at other times you feel anxious, resistant, reactive, and emotionally volatile. On that missed Zoom call, Cameron and I had planned to discuss the ADHD Emotional Health Ladder we had created to help our clients see the dynamic interaction between their ADHD, emotions, and behavior. We believe that if those with ADHD can understand this interplay and be aware of what is happening in their emotional landscape, they will be able to better manage their moment-by-moment situations and make informed choices. Our clients love this conceptual framework because it provides a visual picture for them, making it clear that when they climb or descend a rung in their emotions, they are also shifting their behavior, motivations, traits, and coping mechanisms.

The ADHD Emotional Health Ladder is comprised of five levels: two healthier levels, one average level, and two unhealthy levels. The healthiest traits appear at the top of the ladder. As we descend, we pass progressively through each rung of emotional health. Accurately assessing which rung of the Emotional Ladder we are on helps us observe ourselves and address our behavior.

At each level or rung, our bodies and minds work in particular ways that are either healthy or unhealthy modes of behavior. Just like with the Solve-It Grid, knowing where we are on the Emotional Health Ladder will enable us to work with or through whatever is helping or hindering us. Whether we are aware of it or not, each day we are climbing, resting on, or descending our Emotional Ladder.

By now we know that emotions are real and necessary—especially for those with ADHD—and we need to pay attention to them. When we are at higher health levels on the ladder, we notice those emotions, and they inform us. When we are at the lower levels, they will take over, yelling, kicking, and throwing sand at us to alert us to the extreme danger they presume is around the next corner.

I encourage clients to note what is happening within them on every rung in the following six categories, which are a part of each level on the ladder.

Present and Calm
LEVEL 1

Attending To
LEVEL 2

Autopilot
LEVEL 3

Survival
LEVEL 4

Delusional
LEVEL 5

1. *Awareness* is a sort of radar that operates in the background of our minds and continually scans both the environment outside of us and the state of our internal environment. It's what allows us to notice things around us without focusing exclusively on them.
2. *Attention* refers to our ability to focus on a specific stimulus or stimuli.
3. The *emotional voice* informs us about our inner state. At the lower levels, it is louder and more directive. At the upper levels, it is quieter and acts more as a guide than a dictator.
4. *Body engagement* refers to what is happening to us physiologically.
5. *ADHD symptoms* indicates how our symptoms usually manifest themselves at a particular stage.
6. *Relation to others* describes the ways we are likely to interact with other people while on this rung of the ladder.

You will naturally move up and down in these levels of health daily, weekly, and sometimes hourly. Your goal in using this tool is to notice where you are, increasing your awareness of your emotions so you may better manage yourself.

Level 3: Autopilot

I'm going to begin in the middle at Level 3: Autopilot. Most of us on any given day will find ourselves here. It is called Autopilot because we aren't consciously controlling our thoughts, attitudes, and behaviors. We move through the day by responding to all the urgent needs that appear before us. Although we may not be as strategic in handling them as we could be, we feel productive because we get tasks accomplished.

Level 3: Autopilot

Awareness: We are driven by compulsive, unconscious drives, and our ability to use our radar to assess ourselves and our surroundings is low.

Attention: We make decisions impulsively. The goal is to solve an immediate problem while not necessarily using strategy. Our focus is on action and productivity. We often say and do things to try to gain control over situations that feel chaotic.

Present and Calm
LEVEL 1

Attending To
LEVEL 2

Autopilot
LEVEL 3

Survival
LEVEL 4

Delusional
LEVEL 5

Emotional Voice: The emotional voice is partitioned, usually unsuccessfully, in a "not now" response. The voice isn't really quieted and will burst out if obstacles occur. Emotions are focused around feelings of stress and anxiety.

Body Engagement: We feel the fight-or-flight response, which is a physiological response to stress. Our heart rate increases, our adrenal gland releases cortisol (a stress hormone), and we receive a boost of adrenaline, which increases energy and anxiety. This fight-or-flight response occurs at this level as we look for anything that may be a threat to us.

ADHD Symptoms: We use a fight-or-flight response as a coping mechanism to accomplish tasks. Because we are focused on a quick fix, we are trapped in repetitive and reactive patterns. Our short-term memory is even more unreliable.

Relation to Others: Getting our own way is very important. We are quickly annoyed when people don't meet our expectations. We often look for what we can get from our relationships and aren't really concerned with giving back.

Because of my busy fall schedule, I had unwittingly set myself up to operate on Level 3. My attention was on productivity and seizing the opportunity of the day. My plans were written in concrete and did not allow for variations to the schedule. Although my emotional voice was present and trying to warn me with comments such as, "I might be going too fast. Maybe I should slow down so I can think more clearly," I kept hitting the snooze button on the voice so I could work uninterrupted. As a result, my physical body, ADHD symptoms, and relationships were also affected. Because I was so focused on efficiency, I concentrated narrowly on tasks, ignoring how tired I was and how it affected my marriage.

At Level 3, we are not managing our ADHD symptoms strategically; instead, we are reactive, putting out fires as they occur. Our relationships at Level 3 are functional, with the expectation, "You do your job so that I can do mine." If we are not careful, we will not be fully present with those we love because we are just trying to get the next thing done.

When there is an unanticipated bump in the road, our Level 3 focus on productivity can't handle the transitional thoughts and behaviors needed to adjust for our scheduling errors. We load our plate too full, and our autopilot system breaks down. Emotions flood our mind, and we drop a rung to Level 4.

Level 4: Survival

At this level, we are responsive to our greatest perceived threats. Our emotions start to take over to meet these threats. We begin to employ survival tactics—fight, flight, or freeze—as self-protective responses to our environment. We start to lose the ability to make reasonable choices and become fixated on the survival tactic we have chosen.

Just a few minutes before my text from Cameron with the Zoom link, I had a view of my whole day, but now I could only focus on my mistake. *What do I need to do to fix this error? I have a client*

141

Level 4: Survival

Awareness: Our awareness is reduced to looking for threats. We lack self-awareness and make decisions completely instinctively.

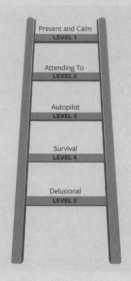

Attention: Because of our focus on survival and getting our basic needs met, we indulge ourselves, physically and emotionally. We often do whatever we feel like doing—even when that isn't the healthiest option.

Emotional Voice: The emotional voice is commandeering. It wants its emotional needs met immediately. Emotions are focused around feelings of fear and anxiety.

Body Engagement: Our body remains on high alert; it eventually adapts and learns how to live with a higher stress level. We won't sleep as well, and we might gain or lose unhealthy amounts of weight.

ADHD Symptoms: Because we are constantly putting out fires, we find ourselves irritable, frustrated, and having poor concentration. Thinking tends to be mostly black-and-white at this stage.

Relation to Others: We are self-centered and very critical of others.

calling in just a few minutes. What do I need to do? My mind scrambled to think. My levels of awareness and attention had changed quickly. And now my emotional voice was yelling at me, calling me stupid, a failure, and other such things.

I texted Cameron my frantic apologies about missing our appointment. As co-creator of the ADHD Emotional Health Ladder, he could see that I was dropping down to the lower rungs. His response text read, "Attach a bungee and get back up. Don't make stuff up about being unreliable. Focus on what is in front of you today. We'll be fine." His empathetic and kind response felt like a breeze on my face.

I took a deep breath. Then another. Then I texted, "Yikes! You got me. I was starting to hit the self-loathing thoughts pretty hard." It was then that I realized I had slipped to Level 4. My shoulders and neck felt tight, and I was breathing with short, quick breaths.

I had one minute before the session with my client was to begin. It wasn't realistic for me to try to climb up the ladder now. Instead, I would need to figure out how to work from where I was. I planned how I would use my coaching skills for the next fifty-five minutes. Then, for the rest of the day, I made the effort to climb from Level 4 back to Level 3.

Level 5: Delusional

There are times when our emotions become even more intense and we are in danger of falling to the next rung, Level 5: Delusional. At this level, we are out of touch with reality. We are uncontrollable, unreasonable, and willing to destroy others and ourselves. Our mind obsessions completely take over our lives. Others may not see just how crazy we feel at this level, but we are certainly aware of it.

On the outside, Hannah looked like she had it together—especially at work. She was a cyber-threat analyst and had a good reputation for her skills in network engineering. She was working with a therapist on her anxiety and depression issues and wanted to address her ADHD symptoms with me. When I sat with her during our first session, she explained that she felt completely out of control in her life. "I am so angry all of the time—mostly at myself. I can't even think straight. I hate my ADHD for making me so incompetent."

Hannah was at Level 5. Her awareness and attention were focused on looking for threats to her emotional safety. Her emotional voice remained relentless, still attempting to motivate her with intense emotions.

Level 5: Delusional

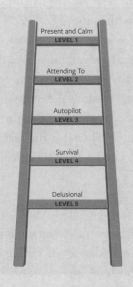

Awareness: Our complete lack of awareness means that our behavior and decisions have the potential to be destructive to ourselves and others.

Attention: Our focus on basic survival causes us to remain on the alert, constantly looking for threats to our emotional safety.

Emotional Voice: The emotional voice is fatigued but keeps screaming demands to have our emotional needs met. Intense emotions prevail in all situations. Fear, depression, and anxiety mark this level, resulting in exhaustion.

Body Engagement: Struggling with stress for long periods has drained our physical, emotional, and mental resources to the point where our body no longer has strength to fight stress. We may feel our situation is hopeless.

ADHD Symptoms: We are emotionally volatile, oversensitive, and oppositional.

Relation to Others: We can be either very clingy or very distant and critical of others. We project our frustration and anger with ourselves onto others.

Present and Calm
LEVEL 1

Attending To
LEVEL 2

Autopilot
LEVEL 3

Survival
LEVEL 4

Delusional
LEVEL 5

Hannah's body was responding to her low level of health. She was quite thin and had numerous food sensitivities, headaches, and digestive issues. She had been to many doctors for a diagnosis, even the Mayo Clinic, but none of them could locate the problem. "I have lost so much time being ill," she said. "I have a problem with relationships. I just broke up with my boyfriend. He told me that I pushed him away and that my extreme emotions were too much for him." She stopped, stared away from me for a moment, and then said, "I know he's right." Hannah was exhausted from being at Level 5 for most of her adult life.

Although Hannah was operating at the bottom of the ladder, there was hope for her to climb up the rungs and to learn how to be emotionally healthy. She wasn't stuck there permanently.

Now that we've seen how low we can go, let's look at what the healthy emotional levels can do for us.

In the two healthier levels of emotionally managing ADHD, people at both ladder rungs are strategic and engage their environment more thoughtfully than at the previously discussed levels. As we ascend the ladder, our awareness and attention increase while our dependence on the emotional voice decreases.

Let's return to Level 3: Autopilot, the place where we are likely to be most of the time. In order to move up the Emotional Health Ladder to Level 2: Attending To, we must ask ourselves, "How can I regulate my emotions? How can I manage ADHD instead of letting it manage me? What strategies can I employ to help me complete tasks more effectively?"

Level 2: Attending To

On Level 2, we are responsive to the most significant tasks without becoming emotionally overwhelmed or hitting snooze on the emotional voice. We have long periods of being present in a nonreactive moment. Emotions inform us rather than dominate us as we make

Level 2: Attending To

Awareness: We're often feeling good and managing our lives, but we don't have the same degree of awareness as Level 1.

Attention: We are more attuned and open to ourselves and our environment.

Emotional Voice: The emotional voice provides good information but isn't taking over by shouting. It informs our awareness.

Body Engagement: Our breathing and posture both relax because we are not in a state of fight-or-flight.

Present and Calm
LEVEL 1

Attending To
LEVEL 2

Autopilot
LEVEL 3

Survival
LEVEL 4

Delusional
LEVEL 5

ADHD Symptoms: Problematic symptoms are identified. Strategies and techniques are key to managing symptoms. They are used carefully and consistently.

Relation to Others: We look for win-win solutions.

decisions. We are more conscious of detracting moments and can keep them under control.

When I am at Level 2: Attending To, I am able to think very differently because my awareness and attention are attuned to my environment. Instead of scanning for threats as I would in the lower levels, I am aware of and attending to what is actually happening. I notice when I need to shift my attention from one task to another. I hear my emotional voice as an informant guiding me: "You might want to watch the next step; it could be tricky." I thank the emotional voice and keep working. It reminded me not to fixate on the technical issue I am having in QuickBooks.

Instead, I make a note to ask my accountant a question and move to the next task. On Level 2, I have more cognitive control over my thoughts.

While on this level, I am breathing at a slow, regular pace, and I don't feel tension anywhere in my body. I remind myself of strategies to employ to keep myself steady and on task, to plan and transition from one task to another. If an unexpected event happens or I realize I have made another mistake on my calendar, I don't immediately fall to Level 4 negative thoughts and behaviors. Instead, I have an emotional margin available to assess, recalculate, and reorient using strategies such as the Solve-It Grid.

I am happy with how I am managing my life when I am at Level 2. I am focused on positive outcomes and am learning and growing. I am in touch with my values and live them out in a positive way.

Level 1: Present and Calm

At this level, we are in a state of perpetual "presence." We have a quiet mind, and we are entirely in touch with the present moment, the now. We have behavioral freedom to respond to tasks, people, and situations the way we would like to respond.

One afternoon, I walked into the waiting area to greet a family that included a nineteen-year-old client, his mother, and his father. The father stepped toward me and introduced himself with a vigorous, tight handshake. Then he stepped even closer. "What makes you qualified to work with us? Who are you? What's your education? What's your training?" His words landed sharply in a staccato rhythm, and his questions continued without giving me a chance to respond.

I was surprised by his aggressiveness. If I had been at a lower level on the Emotional Health Ladder, I would likely have seen his behavior as threatening, been taken aback, and reacted out of emotion. Or, even worse, I would have felt the need to prove to him that I was a good coach. Fortunately, at that moment I was on Level 1. My attention and awareness were focused on remaining in the present and being calm. Because I was attuned to my emotions, I could observe the emotions of others from a distance without getting drawn into them. I didn't see the man as a threat at all.

I had spoken to his wife before this session, and she told me their son was in a challenging situation at school. My emotional voice reasoned that this man was deeply concerned about his son and wanted reassurance that I could help.

Level 1: Present and Calm

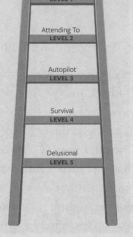

Awareness: We find that we respond as needed to whatever life presents, actualizing the positive potentials.

Attention: We become more present and focused on what is actually happening around us. We are not fixated on defensive thoughts.

Emotional Voice: We are attuned to our emotions. The emotional voice provides important guidance for us.

Body Engagement: We feel more present and awake in our mind, heart, and body.

ADHD Symptoms: Symptoms are still present but are met with mindfulness, problem solving, and planning.

Relation to Others: We respect and value relationships and regularly demonstrate this by our words and actions.

I paused and considered my next action. "Of course you have questions!" I said in a smooth and encouraging voice. "Let's go back to a coaching room and discuss those." My nonreactive response and invitation seemed to calm him.

If I hadn't been at Level 1, I wouldn't have been able to manage my surprise when he stepped into my personal space and intensely questioned me. The entire session would have gone quite differently. I may have missed hearing and sensing the frustration they were all experiencing.

After a good session, the father shook my hand and thanked me for listening to his family. "I know that you can help us," he said.

Because I was operating at Level 1, the family was able to leave feeling hopeful rather than frustrated and discouraged.

Level 1: Present and Calm is the ideal place for us to be as we work with our ADHD symptoms, yet it is not realistic for us to expect to be there all of the time.

I found myself clenching my toes and grinding my teeth as I watched the award-winning film *Free Solo*, documenting Alex Honnold's incredibly dangerous free climb (climbing without any ropes or protective measures) of El Capitan in Yosemite Valley. Even though I knew that Honnold would be alive at the end of the documentary, I was scared for him the entire time. If he fell, there was nothing to catch him. It would inevitably be a fatal fall to the base of the three-thousand-foot monolith. During Honnold's final push to the top, my palms got increasingly sweaty from the images on my screen and the knowledge of the incredible risk. By the time it was over, I was emotionally drained and rattled.

Honnold had climbed El Capitan countless times before attempting his free solo. He knew every inch of that rock face so well that he could draw images of it from memory. While climbing, he always knew exactly where he was on that rock wall. That knowledge helped him make wise decisions along the way.

The ADHD Ladder of Emotional Health is intended to help you place where you are on the "rock wall" of your ADHD emotional landscape at all times. It is my hope that this knowledge will help you know which decisions you need to make to progress in a healthy upward direction. It gives you a framework to examine the interplay among your awareness, attention, emotions, signals in your body, ADHD symptoms, and relationships with others. It can help you reflect on your emotions and actions while orienting you so you can better manage yourself and your emotions.

11

Welcome Home

Creating Healthy Boundaries

His name was Michael. A sweet-hearted junior in high school, he was also a close talker. He stood what felt like inches from my face, and I could feel a light sprinkle as he asked about his homework assignment.

"Michael," I said with a smile. "Remember the bubble?" I made a circular motion around my body. Without pausing, he quickly stepped back. He never remembered the bubble boundary, so I reminded him each day of the academic year. I didn't mind, because it was my boundary to uphold.

Boundaries are rules we set for ourselves, based on our values and priorities. They are the physical, emotional, and mental limits we establish to protect ourselves from being spit on, or being manipulated, used, or violated by others. They also exist to keep our individual selves separate from others.

Some boundaries are automatically in place without us having to be consciously aware of them. Although I was only a first-year teacher when I had Michael in my class, I could plainly see my physical-boundary bubble with students. At the time, though, I hadn't really thought through what my other boundaries should be. My twenty-something self had yet to learn that setting boundaries is essential to emotional health. If we don't know what our limits are, we can't enforce them.

Like so many others with ADHD, I had poor boundaries in almost every area of my life. I didn't learn good boundaries from either of my parents. Their ADHD went undiagnosed, and they didn't set healthy limits for themselves or me.

Most of my clients struggle with boundaries. Our family of origin, ADHD symptoms, coping mechanisms, and rejection sensitivity all work against us. Our symptoms (lack of self-regulation, impulsivity, fluctuating moods) make it challenging to set and enforce boundaries. Some of us even fail to remember to respect other people's parameters. Our coping mechanisms, which include people pleasing and shaming ourselves, also interfere with our ability to set reasonable limits. And many with ADHD have what is called rejection sensitive dysphoria (RSD). Those who have RSD don't want to set boundaries because they are deeply afraid of being rejected.

Though boundary setting is difficult, it is vital for a healthy life. Taking responsibility for yourself by setting healthy perimeters is how you can increase your self-regulation and manage your ADHD.

The house-yard-fence analogy has helped many of my clients create more explicit boundaries for their thoughts and relationships. Using this analogy will help you think about the guidelines you have set for your life and identify areas where changes will increase your emotional health.

The House

Think of your internal self—your psyche and personhood—as a house. It's yours alone. No one is allowed to come in unless you have given them permission. It is an intimate space where no family members or close friends have the right to intrude. Not even the God of the universe will enter unless you allow him to.[1] You can give them permission to enter, and you can ask them to leave whenever you want. You are the only one who can live there because there is only room for one. This house represents your most profound sense of self. You, and only you, get to choose what happens in this house.

You decorate the place as you wish. You paint the walls with colors that please you and place photos on the walls that remind you of good times or of your ideal self. In this house, you create your identity—your qualities, values, beliefs, and personality.

This is also the place where you work on yourself. You need to do what you can to keep the house as clutter free as possible—clean a closet, sort out old memories and other emotional knickknacks that you have acquired. You may have boxes hidden in rooms that contain remnants of traumatic injuries and pain—emotional as well as physical. Perhaps someday those heavy boxes will get opened with the help of a professional, but for now, they are locked away. It's your house, and when you are ready, you will tend to those darkened, dusty spaces.

Doing the Housework

Boundaries help you monitor your own behavior and create a healthy structure for your life. They keep you from eating French fries at every meal or staying up until 2:00 a.m. when you have to be at work at 7:00. Setting boundaries for yourself is like doing housework in your metaphorical house. Because you respect your own home, you can set guidelines for keeping it in running order. You decide your house rules when you determine, "Here's the line between what works for me and what doesn't work for me. Here's the line that I won't cross." The idea is to make rules that keep you safe and healthy and keep your life running smoothly.

Everyone's boundaries in their house are unique. The limits you create for yourself will reflect *your* needs and priorities. Do you need to set physical boundaries? They won't be precisely the same as the list below, but these will give you an idea of what physical boundaries or limits for yourself might look like:

- keeping a regular bedtime and wake-up time
- sticking to your budget
- not having screens (television, phone) in your bedroom
- not working past 7:00 p.m.
- not answering work emails on the weekends
- buying only what's on your shopping list (i.e., no impulse buys at Target)
- doing laundry every Friday
- not checking Instagram every time you're bored
- eating out no more than twice a week
- brushing your teeth
- not drinking alcohol on weeknights
- not keeping junk food in the house
- limiting yourself to two cups of coffee per day

Excited by the idea of getting their house in order, some of my clients make a long list of changes. But because the list is so long, they become overwhelmed and don't carry out any of them. Begin organizing your house by choosing only one or two of the basic limits.

I began with one simple rule for myself—to keep my car tidy. I decided to clean out the trash each time I filled up the gas tank. It's such a simple thing to do, yet it has made a big difference in managing the mess in my car. After that, when the boundary became a habit that I could perform without thinking about it, I added a new guideline for myself.

Boundaries with Emotions

Sometimes our housework has more to do with setting emotional limits on ourselves. Where is your emotional baggage stored in your house? Are there boxes filled with hurt, anger, fear, and anxiety cluttering the hallway? Are there discarded, broken pieces of furniture representing sadness, envy, or shame scattered about your living room? Maybe it's time to rid your house of those things that clutter your otherwise neat home.

Blake examined his house. He began by looking at the item in his home that most bothered him. "I have a room where I keep all my envy. It's like I've stacked old newspapers everywhere. It's not really messing up my metaphorical living space, but I come across piles every once in a while. Last weekend, a friend of mine bought a cottage. And instead of being happy for him, I felt jealous. It was as though I was adding another stack of newspapers to my living area." He paused, considering. "Those old newspapers aren't valuable or helpful. I'll feel better getting rid of them." He realized that after he cleared out the trash, he could use that space for healthier emotions.

Blake had a mental picture of his envy. It took several months for him to sort through his old newspapers and toss most of them out. When he is tempted to want what a friend has, he reminds himself, "That's just a newspaper. I don't want or need to hold on to it anymore." Then he imagines stepping out of his house into his yard to congratulate his friend.

Shame is another item found in many ADHD houses. Theresa's house was full of it. "I guess you could call me a shame hoarder." Her childhood had been a rough one. She grew up believing that she was somehow bad and not worthy of love. "I mean, I get it here." She pointed to her head. "I know that I am worthy of being loved. But I don't get it here." And she placed her hand to her heart. She felt the persistent emotional burden of not being good enough. She was a shame collector.

Theresa began to search her house for shame elements and discovered that shame wasn't tucked in some hideaway; it was everywhere. She imagined that ghosts haunted her house and whispered lies, such as, "Why did you go and ruin everything?" and "You are a hopeless loser." These lies were especially vocal and vicious about her ADHD mistakes, like forgetting to pay a bill.

"Once I started hearing the judging words in my house, I knew that I needed to get them out," she said. When I asked her what she did to get rid of them, she smiled. "I'm from the Midwest. We're polite people. I respectfully asked those ghosts to leave." Then she added, "Oh, they come back sometimes, and I ask them to leave again." It took focus and persistence for her to take charge of her home and what was allowed in it.

How can you set emotional boundaries for yourself? Maybe you can spot behaviors that cause you to collect unwanted items or trash before they are allowed to set up residence in your house. Here are some examples of limits that you may want to consider applying as you clean your house:

- not participating in gossip or talking about someone behind their back
- avoiding people who are hurtful, who stress you out, etc.
- not lying to get out of trouble
- not blaming others but instead taking responsibility for your own actions

Be compassionate with yourself as you learn to manage your home. It's counterproductive to expect perfection and to blast yourself for not keeping all of your boundaries firm. When you struggle with an area of your home, be gentle with yourself. Being too harsh or unrealistic leads to more shame, more hopelessness, and giving up. Explore the reasons for the clutter being there in the first place, then clean the best that you can. Adjust your boundaries so you don't pick up more unwanted mess.

Before Moving On

Describe your house. What do you need to do to maintain it? What repairs are needed? What is in the boxes cluttering your heart? Are they boxes of grudges, hurts, failures, shame, or envy? When do you plan on cleaning them out? What is the first step to begin that process? Have you let someone into your house who doesn't belong there and needs to be evicted?

The Yard

Outside your house you have a yard. This is the space where special friends and loved ones gather. These are the folks you want to spend time with—people to whom you will send invitations for a grill-out and a party but who are not quite intimate enough to allow into your house. The people you invite into your yard are those you can trust to respect and appreciate this green space you have created and to help when you need it. When asked, they offer their opinions on plantings, maintenance, or the colorful gnomes you have placed around the yard. Yet they understand that they are only guests. They may offer opinions and suggestions, but ultimately it is your choice whether or not to accept their feedback.

Creating Your Yard

Dawn was going through a divorce when she learned the importance of creating a yard. "I spent years without a yard. I was hiding—protecting myself and wanting to seem like I had everything together—so I didn't tell anyone about my fractured, painful reality." As a result, she was alone. "I lacked the support system I needed when it came time to make difficult choices."

Two years later, she now has a clear understanding of what she wants her growing yard to look like and who belongs in it. "Cultivating my yard taught me about evaluating friendships and honoring myself in the process. It gave me the gift of some amazing friends when I needed them most."

Just like your house, your yard consists of two major elements: a space that best serves you and your emotional growth and health, and what or who is allowed there. When you create your yard, create a space that allows for joy, rest, recreation, and, when necessary, hard work. Choose people to invite into this space whom you trust to care for you and who want to support you. They should have your best interests in mind. Be honest with yourself and others about your needs and expectations. Understand that they are fluid and can change from day to day. Today you may need more laughter than advice. Tomorrow you may need that advice or just a listening ear. The following day you may want to just hang out.

Once you have created a yard and invited trusted people to join you, you get to define your boundaries and be clear about what is acceptable in your yard and what isn't. It takes time and effort to think about appropriate boundaries. To create great yard boundaries, you can clearly express the expectations you have for your guests and what good behavior looks like. These boundaries will include physical, emotional, mental, and spiritual parameters.

Only institute rules you're willing to enforce. If you tell your chronically late friend that you'll wait for them for twenty minutes, and you're still there when they show up forty-five minutes late, you've failed to hold to a boundary crossing. Don't ruminate about how your friend should have known that you'd be angry they were so late. You're the one who set a boundary of twenty minutes and then didn't protect it.

Yard boundaries do not require apology or justification. They are your boundaries. Period. An unhealthy person will defy or mock your boundaries and try to make you feel stupid for having set them, whereas a healthy "yard person" may ask questions to clarify but will accept your boundaries without feeling affronted.

Enforcing Yard Boundaries

Once your boundaries are clear and set in place, that's where the yard work can get tough. When someone is misbehaving in your yard, it needs to be dealt with right away.

Pam's mother-in-law reorganized her (actual, not metaphorical) kitchen, her closets, and the kids' rooms while she was babysitting Pam's children. "It felt like she was coming into my yard and ripping out the daffodils I planted because she didn't like them." As Pam said this, she felt the sting of anger. Then she added, "I need to come up with a way of addressing that in the future. It's my yard, for heaven's sake."

She decided to use the "here's what happened and here's what I expected" approach. She sat with her mother-in-law and explained what she experienced, how it affected her, and what she hoped for in the future. Her mother-in-law, because she was a true yard person for Pam, responded well and explained that she thought she was helping the busy family, but she would respect that line in the future. They grew closer as a result of this discussion.

But sometimes people in your yard aren't willing or able to have the healthy discussions that Pam and her mother-in-law had. Dawn realized that sad truth with her mother. "Unfortunately, I learned that my mom has no respect for my yard. Her criticism isn't constructive; it tears me down. She's mean." Dawn had assumed that her mom would be in her yard because they are related. Now she sees that her mom came into her space and acted destructively in it. Dawn did her yard work and expressed healthy guidelines to her mother, and still her mother repeatedly and flagrantly disregarded them.

When your boundaries are crossed, you must respond. It's common to resent people when they cross your boundaries, but resentment comes from helplessness. And you have options—you are not helpless. Sometimes we kick people out of our yard prematurely in the mistaken belief that there are no other options.

The first option is to talk about the infraction with that person. You can say things like, "I didn't feel comfortable when you said/ did that." Or, "I would rather you didn't talk to others about _____. That information was meant to be kept between us." Or, "Here is the boundary I instituted between us, and your actions crossed that line. I think we need to talk about it."

Explore your options before booting someone out of the yard for good. Like Pam and her mother-in-law, you may find a stronger relationship after an honest, kind discussion. Make sure you've done your own work before giving up on others. If the thought of removing people from your yard causes you fear, it's likely you need to manage your reaction to *their* emotional response.

Childhood traumas and injuries can affect how we approach others when our boundaries are violated. Please remember that you were helpless as a child during those events. However, now that you are an adult, you are no longer helpless. You have personal power, options, and recourse. Don't shy away from using them responsibly in caring for your house and yard.

It is your job to let people know how to act in your yard, and when they don't respect your space, they need to go. Guests are never allowed to destroy your bushes, ruin your garden, or break things. You will find that unhealthy people tend not to respect yard space and do not like the boundaries that others set. They unapologetically make changes, criticize, or are destructive. If they refuse to accept your guidelines or respect your ideas, or, worse, they mock you for having boundaries for your yard, it is a clear indication that they are not supposed to be there. If this is the case, it is time to use the fence.

Before Moving On

Describe your yard. What have you intentionally designed it for? How do you continually improve it? Who is in it? How do you know that the right people are in it? What are your yard rules? Are there any difficult conversations you need to have?

The Fence

Imagine a fence around your yard. Most of the world is on the other side of that enclosure. It helps delineate where our yard begins and free access to us ends. Although I was taken aback by the woman who "helped" me by taking my glass off the podium because she thought I would forget it, she was on the outside of my fence. I could reframe the situation as someone who tried to help in an awkward way. However, if she had been one of my yard people, I would have taken the opportunity to explain that while I appreciate reminders, I feel insulted when people just assume that I will forget something or make a mistake because of my ADHD. And because they are my yard people and want the best for me, they would understand.

When I ask clients to visualize their fence, their responses can often tell me if there is a problem with their property line. For example, Nicole noticed that she felt so desperate to have people in her yard that she had a meager string delineating her boundary line. "I feel like I'm handing out flyers advertising for anyone to enter." We needed to work on her yard rules and who should be in her yard.

David, on the other hand, envisioned a thick stone wall that was twenty feet high. When I asked how people entered his yard, he shrugged, "They don't." As we talked, he explained how he used to let people into his yard, but they hadn't behaved well, and now it was just easier to build a very thick, high wall. He and I worked on lowering his barrier and creating a gate for a special few to enter.

When you have asked people to leave and they keep coming back to attempt access, you have to be firm with stronger boundaries. It is not rude to ignore unwanted texts or phone calls. It is okay not to answer personal questions from nosy or even truly interested coworkers. You are not obligated to those outside your fence who are requesting or pushing for closer access.

Your fence generally needs to be created with more than a piece of string and less than a thick stone wall. You do, however, need a fence that is easily identified as a barrier so that others can see it.

Sometimes those who tend to ruin your yard need to temporarily stay outside the fence. Sometimes those people are family members. Sometimes they are friends. Sometimes that person is your spouse. It doesn't mean you are angry with them, and it doesn't mean you can't interact with them. Maybe you bring drinks to them at the fence line. You enjoy the conversation, but you can leave when you need to. There is a space between you and them that provides rest and safety. They cannot uproot your bushes, ruin your flowers, or break things in your home from that distance.

I can still show love, appreciation, and care for people on the other side of my fence. It's just that not everyone is invited into my yard for more in-depth discussions and experiences.

Before Moving On

What does your fence look like? Do you have the right kind? Can others identify it as a fence? How do you know when you can let someone from the other side of the fence into your yard?

Healthy home-yard-fence understandings and boundaries bring us self-confidence and self-respect and lead to higher productivity, more energy, and overall happiness. Take the time to delineate the guidelines on your property, and then uphold the rules you set with your actions. Don't let boundary violations slide. When you do these things, you'll take greater control of your ADHD and the rest of your life by creating respect for yourself and others.

12

Dancing through the Day

Hacks for Adulting

Jada sat with me, her notebook on her lap. The cover read, *Pretending to Be a Normal Person Day After Day Is Exhausting*. She was the type of person who didn't try to hide her ADHD but instead embraced it as a significant cognitive difference. She waved her hands as she explained, "I tried shoving my pesky ADHD traits into a closet, but it was too tiring, and they kept coming out anyway." Her long, dark curls bobbed, animating her words. "I realized that over the long haul, pretending to be 'normal' is exhausting and comes at a dangerously high cost to my self-worth and even my health."

Jada had come such a long way in managing her ADHD. She had worked for a couple of years on her emotional regulation. She had become aware of what was holding her attention, what was happening around her, and how her emotional voice was influencing her in the moment. But she knew she had more work to do. "I need to figure out how to hack adulting." She wanted to work on ways to address being successful in her daily routines. Instead of adopting many little strategies to help her, we focused on three practical ways that she could help herself—managing her sleep, protecting her peak times, and learning to rehearse.

Managing Sleep

I asked Jada about her sleep habits. She grimaced. "I already know what you're going to say."

I grinned. My clients know that I push only one agenda item: sleep. Sufficient sleep is a crucial part of physical and mental well-being for all humans. Getting a good night's rest can be incredibly difficult for those with ADHD. Nearly all of my clients have some sort of sleep problem: difficulty falling asleep, experiencing restful sleep, staying asleep, or waking up from their slumber.

Sleep is difficult for many reasons. For example, for more than 80 percent of those with ADHD, the sleep cycles are flipped.[1] Instead of sleeping deeply in one of the first two sleep cycles like their neurotypical counterparts, they wake up multiple times until about 4:00 a.m. Then they fall into "the sleep of the dead," from which they have extreme difficulty rousing themselves. Because of their deep sleep, many of my clients describe sleeping through two or three alarms, as well as the attempts of family members to get them out of bed.

After Jada acknowledged that she knew she didn't get enough sleep, we talked about how difficult elusive sleep can be when one has ADHD. "Well, it's not exactly that," she said. "I don't even like to sleep."

I hear three false beliefs frequently:

- "Sleep is a waste of time."
- "I don't need a lot of sleep."
- "It's just too hard to get to sleep."

Jada had many things to do during the day in her busy life, and she loved her late-night quiet time. Her kids were in bed then, and like a little elf, she crept around her house doing the tasks that she loved. Eventually, Jada reasoned that sleep was a waste of time. She explained, "Night is the only time that I have to myself. So of course I will choose to stay awake instead of sleeping."

Like Jada, clients who hold this belief often describe themselves as night owls who get a burst of energy when the sun goes down. They question the necessity of sleep.

The truth is that scientists have identified a vital brain-cleaning function that occurs mostly when your brain is at rest. When you're asleep, a waste-clearance system in the body, known as the glymphatic system, runs what is essentially a rinse cycle in the brain, using cerebrospinal fluid (the clear liquid found in the brain and spine). Experts believe that this fluid flows more freely through the brain when it rests during the night.[2] During this time, it washes away a harmful protein known as beta-amyloid. When this process doesn't occur, scientists believe that beta-amyloid can build up, forming the plaques that are characteristic of Alzheimer's disease. Sleep is necessary.

Another false belief I often hear from my clients is that they don't need a lot of sleep. Clients refer to legends like Albert Einstein or Benjamin Franklin, who allegedly did not sleep more than four hours a night. The truth is that most adults require between seven and nine hours of nightly sleep.[3] The folklore around those who did not sleep much is usually exaggeration or a result of physiological disturbance. Research strongly implies that people who regularly get fewer than six hours of sleep are at higher risk for diabetes, heart disease, stroke, cognitive decline, and death from any cause.[4] A lack of restful sleep also makes it more likely that a person will gain weight and have higher stress-hormone cortisol levels.

Finally, some of my clients are so frustrated with their lack of sleep that they come to the conclusion that they simply can't sleep. They say in desperation, "It's too hard to get to sleep. I try and try, but I can't. I just can't do it." About three-fourths of all adults with ADHD report the inability to shut off their mind so they can fall asleep at night. Others tell me that they feel tired throughout the day, but their mind clicks on as soon as their head hits the pillow. Their thoughts jump or bounce from one worry to another. Through this real experience for my clients, their false belief tells them that there is nothing they can do about their elusive sleep.

Though it can be challenging to fall asleep, there are many things that you can do to help yourself. It takes about forty-five minutes for you to slow down your brain. During the period leading up to bedtime, purposefully signal to your mind and body that you will be ending your day and resting soon. Dim the lights in your environment. Slow your breathing. Decrease your physical movements. This is a great time to do nonaddictive Blue tasks on the Solve-It Grid. Recognize all the things that foster true relaxation and quiet for you.

When it is time to fall asleep, consider conditions that will help you move in that direction. Some people need absolute silence. Others need white noise, such as a fan or radio, to mask disturbances to sleep. Some people need a snack before bed, while others can't eat anything at that time. I sleep best in a cold, dark room with the covers piled high.

Not getting enough sleep or wanting to sleep at times that don't coordinate with school or work obligations can have significant long-term effects: physical illness, behavioral issues, and mood changes. Improving sleep quality can reduce ADHD problems and positively impact you and your family's everyday lives. When you get enough sleep, you are more able to work efficiently during the day.

Protecting Peak Times

Can you name certain times of day when you do your best work—when you feel a high level of focus, attention, and efficiency? Think of the hours between 6:00 a.m. and 8:00 p.m. My peak hours are between 8:30 and 11:30 a.m. This is my most productive time. I protect it by not scheduling meetings or doing things that don't require my full energy. I find peak time is the prime time to accomplish those troublesome but important Yellow tasks on my list.

Take your own energy rhythms into account when planning your day, and understand that, realistically, you will be effective at certain times of the day more than others. Generally, it takes a few hours after waking up in the morning for you to reach peak alertness and energy. A circadian dip causing sleepiness occurs from approximately 1:00 to 3:00 p.m., especially when you haven't slept enough the night before.

Many of my clients believe that they are most productive between 1:00 and 3:00 a.m. Though they *feel* that they are accomplishing a lot, when I probe into their accomplishments, they are usually lackluster. Either very little is completed, or the clients were easily distracted. After examining their pattern, they agree that their productivity was more of a nighttime illusion than an effective method of task accomplishment.

Try to find a natural rhythm to your day and keep that rhythm. Jada used the Solve-It Grid as she worked through her daily patterns. "I get to work around eight in the morning, but I'm not really fully awake yet, so I check my email and begin to set up my day. From there, I work on little things here and there. I even chat with my coworkers." As you can see, Jada likes a slow start to her day. "But at ten o'clock, I am at my best," she said. "I close my office door and place a sign on it saying that I am available to talk after 12:00 p.m." Jada told me that she has also learned to notice when her medication for ADHD kicks in. "I feel calm and focused. My thoughts seem to slow down so that I can do all of those Yellow tasks that require mental energy."

She no longer felt guilty when, in the afternoon, she went to a Blue or Green activity at work because she knew that she had maximized her peak time and accomplished her Yellow tasks. Jada was pleased with her pattern. "Instead of trudging through my day, I dance. I know when to expect tempo changes, and I go with it."

Learning to Rehearse

They are officially known as the US Navy Flight Demonstration Squadron. But most of us know them as the Blue Angels, a flight demonstration team. They delight an estimated eleven million spectators each year with their precision and aerobatic maneuvers. During one of their complicated flight formations, the Diamond 360 maneuver, they fly their supersonic jets and place their wingtips within eighteen inches of each other while soaring at 700 miles per hour.

As you may have guessed, they are a highly organized team. They have a particular method to prepare for their extraordinary feats. For every practice and on every show day, the group meets two hours before flying. In their full gear, they sit in the briefing room without any distractions and get focused as a team. The leader begins the briefing talking about the weather, and the group closes their eyes and imagines flying their jets. These expert pilots must look absurd as they grip the imaginary control stick with their right hand and the throttle with their left while they "chair fly" through the maneuvers just like they're flying the plane. Their mental rehearsal technique helps them connect to the flight course as well as to each other.

Mental rehearsal for us nonpilots means that we imagine ourselves doing a particular task to improve the outcome when we do it for real. Visualization techniques like this are widely used among people who are focused on achieving their peak performance in whatever area they want to excel in. We can easily imagine the technique of rehearsing being used by athletes, musicians, artists, and actors. Speakers, teachers, and lawyers rehearse before they present. But this rehearsal can also be used to enhance performance in the office, the home, or anywhere it's applied.

Mental rehearsal is not positive self-talk or imagining scenes that make us feel good. Instead, it is carefully picturing ourselves going through routines. Whether it's precision flying, Olympic figure skating, or something much more mundane like our daily schedule, rehearsal improves our chances of success. It works because our unconscious mind is impacted by repetition and practice as though the activity is actually taking place.

Thankfully, my daily duties don't require the accuracy that the Blue Angels do. However, I use their chair-flying technique as I prepare for my day. While still lying in bed, I look at my calendar on my phone. I take a deep breath and imagine myself going through each step of my day until noon. This includes my morning routine: showering, drying my hair, putting in my contacts, eating breakfast, etc. I rehearse my scheduled sessions: I envision my client's face, hear their voice, and feel the connection with them. I listen to myself beginning the session with them: "What do you want to accomplish in this session?" I walk through the actions and attitudes that I want for that part of the day. Then at lunch, I repeat the process, which takes me to 5:00. And then at 5:00, I will rehearse the evening.

Rehearsing is a crucial strategy for me. When I don't rehearse, I might dread the upcoming events of the day, and I tend to gravitate to my usual ways of thinking, feeling, and acting in my normal ADHD state of mind and body, which tends to be frazzled. (On the ADHD Emotional Health Ladder, that would be Level 3: Autopilot.) On the days when I rehearse successfully, my schedule flows smoothly. I am able to anticipate many events throughout my day, and the office runs on schedule. I feel present and alert. If something unexpected happens, I can accommodate it and remain flexible. On the days when I don't take the time to rehearse, I look and feel harried and hassled, and I often make mistakes with my schedule.

Mental rehearsal works on two levels for me. It strengthens specific behaviors like preparing for transitions in my day, and it helps me reinforce my sense of direction and aligns me with my values.

Unfortunately, most of us with ADHD have learned to use mental rehearsal to practice the exact behaviors we would rather avoid. Jada told me how she used mental rehearsal in a hazardous way. Her supervisor had asked her at the last minute to give a presentation to twenty-five of her colleagues. She had two hours to prepare, and she began to mentally rehearse all the things that could go wrong. Instead of calmly imagining her steps to prepare for the event, her mind raced with doomsday thoughts: *You haven't had enough time to prepare. Someone may ask you a question and you won't know the answer. You may stumble over your words. You are going to look nervous. Your face might freeze on Zoom. You'll lose your train of thought.* She was unconsciously preparing her mind to expect failure. So when she did stumble over her words, her mind took over and she slid to Level 4: Survival. The presentation slowly descended into the negative situation she had imagined as she made mistake after mistake after mistake.

Jada focused so hard on everything going wrong and mentally rehearsed that exact situation so that it played out quickly in reality. She used mental rehearsal to program her unconsciousness to fail. To make matters worse, experiencing a real-life example of failure further reinforced her "I stink at presentations" mentality.

After some work, she learned how to use mental rehearsal to help rather than hinder herself. The next time her supervisor asks her to present to twenty-five of her colleagues, Jada has a plan. She predicts that she will initially feel startled by the assignment, so she plans to take slow, deep breaths as her supervisor speaks. Back in her office, she closes her eyes and breathes slowly, calming herself. She shifts her emotional thoughts to cognitive ones and asks herself, "What steps will I need to take to create a successful presentation?" She opens her eyes and writes down what she will need to do. Feeling overwhelmed, she slows her breathing and closes her eyes again. Her mental rehearsal jumps ahead to the presentation. She sees herself presenting the topic on the virtual platform at her desk. She feels the chair cushion against her back;

she looks in the camera on the computer; she hears the steadiness and confidence in her voice. Jada opens her eyes and remembers that she already knows what needs to be said in this presentation. Her goal for the next hour will be to organize the material.

"It really works!" Jada said. "I calm my mind and focus on how I can accomplish what I need to." She enhanced her focus and reframed her presentation from risk and embarrassment and moved toward fulfilling her professional responsibility.

It doesn't matter what your situation is. You can vividly evoke visual rehearsal, shift your emotional state, reframe the challenge, and rehearse desired actions. When you repeatedly rehearse as Jada did, you build new neural pathways in your brain and new, positive patterns of behavior. Without mental rehearsal, you remain stuck in old action patterns. Every outstanding performance—in the theater, on the playing field, or in just getting through the day successfully—is preceded by rehearsal. Develop strategies that work for you. Identify the problem and let your creativity help you solve it.

When you have ADHD, you are more likely to struggle to accomplish simple tasks in life. Adulting your way through your day can feel overwhelming, chaotic, and out of control until you figure out the keys to your management. Instead of cloaking your ADHD lifestyle or trying to pass it off as normal, create ADHD-friendly ways to move through your life more purposefully. Focus on finding a rhythm through your day and into the evening. Getting enough sleep, protecting your peak work times, and rehearsing upcoming events will help you find a balance as you dance through your day.

The Island of Misfit Toys

Parenting the ADHD Child

"I feel like I am on the Island of Misfit Toys," my daughter Brooke told me as we cuddled, watching the 1964 stop-motion version of *Rudolph the Red-Nosed Reindeer*. The gatekeeper, a Charlie-in-the-Box, had just popped out of his cube and was explaining to the young reindeer and his new friends that they had landed on the Island of Misfit Toys. A menagerie of darling but slightly different toys danced around. Several toys made us smile: a spotted elephant, a train with square wheels on its caboose, a bird that swims instead of flies, a cowboy who rides an ostrich, and a winged bear.

My daughter was in second grade, and it was becoming apparent that school would be difficult for her. She wasn't a *broken* toy, disrespectful or unruly. Instead, she was a lot like the water pistol that squirted jelly in the movie. She was a *misfit* toy who did not seem to fit others' expectations. She consistently missed her teacher's cues and paid for it with verbal scolding and points taken away. Instead of loving recess like other children, she hated it. She felt completely overwhelmed in the hallway, watching her friends scurry to put on their snow pants and winter gear before racing outside for play. She forgot and lost oh so many things at school and at home. Her observation about being on the Island of Misfit Toys confirmed to me that all of the negative attention was beginning to take a toll on her.

Children with ADHD know they are different, and this is rarely experienced as a good thing. They often develop low self-esteem because they realize they make mistakes, like not finishing what they start, misunderstanding directions, or losing their mittens for the fifth time that winter. And because children make no distinction between what they do and who they are, they often feel less capable than their peers. Like the toy bird that swims instead of flies, children with ADHD often feel unwanted because they are different.

I sat on the couch and hugged my little girl. I remembered that when I was her age, I had often wondered how my classmates just knew what to do and when to do it. I noticed that they knew when to turn in papers or begin packing up for the end of the day. I always felt like I was missing something or was a step behind. I reasoned, much like Brooke did, that I was somehow a misfit.

Shame developed from those thoughts. First, shame's voice was a helping little prompt nudging me to remember to write my name in the upper right-hand corner. As the years went on, though, the gentle prods turned to jabs of self-loathing. I didn't want my daughter to feel like this too. It wasn't worth trying to convince her otherwise. She knew that she was a misfit toy while she was at school.

Instead of challenging her feelings, I wanted her to know that she wasn't alone. "I feel like that too sometimes, kiddo," I said. "It's a good thing that we're together on our island. We have each other, and we can figure things out." She didn't need me to fix the toy; she needed me to be with her on the island.

Raising emotionally healthy children who have ADHD is challenging. For a decade I have worked with families who are affected by ADHD. The children who do the best, who grow up to be the most emotionally healthy and resilient adults, have parents who have guided them in specific ways. They raise their children to have an authentic and healthy relationship with them. They teach their children the power of self-efficacy and resiliency. Children with ADHD can grow up to be confident adults if given the necessary nurturing and skills.

Relationship Matters Most

Although it's tempting to focus on micromanaging and organizing your ADHD child, teaching your child how to perform executive functions isn't the most important role you play in their life. The most significant thing you can do for your child is to create a strong, healthy relationship with them. There are four characteristics that create that relationship: endless empathy, trusting respect, stubborn love, and gentle honesty.

Endless empathy is without a doubt the most essential quality healthy parents have when raising an ADHD child. They are able to put themselves into their child's shoes (or heart), and therefore they can tune into the child's deepest feelings and understand their body language.

Because an ADHD child often has big, untamed emotions, empathy can help you not to take it personally when they say mean words in the midst of a meltdown. Having endless empathy for your child doesn't mean that you don't have boundaries for their behavior; it means that you see their pain, anger, and frustration as real. And just as you would like for someone to acknowledge your feelings, so do they.

The best parents seem to know that *trusting respect* goes both ways in relationships. They modify and shape their own behaviors so that they are trustworthy to their children. Treating loved ones with dignity, affirming their worth, and respecting their boundaries and limitations are part of the modeling needed for children to develop respect for themselves and others.

A child needs to be treated with respect in order to develop self-respect. When a parent asks the question, "How can I make my kid behave?" I surmise that there is little respect in the home. Parents who apply trusting respect do not need to boss, force, or lecture their child. Instead, their approach to correcting behavior relies on the relationship they have created as they problem-solve with their child for better outcomes in the future. Both the parent and the child work toward solutions and try new strategies. Children gain confidence as they become the problem solvers capable of managing their lives.

All parents need to love their children, but *feeling* loved is critical for children who feel like a misfit toy. Loving children with a stubborn sort of love means that they can't do anything that will make you love them less. The reverse is also true: they can't do anything that will make you love them more. Your love for them is permanent, and you let them know that each day. Children who grow up with parents who have practiced *stubborn love* are much more confident.

"I feel so guilty," a mom told me. "I really don't like my daughter at all." Her daughter was living at rock bottom: stealing from the family, dealing drugs, and doing other behaviors that accompany that lifestyle.

So many parents confess they don't like their child. Not liking your child's behavior doesn't mean that you've stopped loving your child. The pain from not liking your child comes from the fact that you love them so much. If you didn't love them, you would be apathetic to their behavior.

Stubborn love is a gift to a child with ADHD who feels like a misfit toy. A parent's love provides a shelter for them in a world that feels unsafe. A child who knows that home is a safe place develops a sense that they are lovable and will grow up to accept themselves. Stubborn love refuses to give up hope for the child and remains constant when the child expresses the ugliest of emotions.

The healthiest families with whom I have worked also practice *gentle honesty*. They create a home where feedback (not criticism or lecture) is seen as formative and needed for growth. The parents of these families have developed a specific method for giving timely feedback to everyone in the house. They wait until the emotional storm surge passes and provide calm moments to reflect on changes that need to be made. There is a focus on management of feelings and actions and on developing better responses for the future.

There are undoubtedly other characteristics of creating a strong relationship with your ADHD child that I have left out. Still, I think these form a solid foundation. Be an example of these characteristics in your family. We've all seen our children mimic our daily behaviors: pretending to type on a computer like Mom does or sighing wearily when they see a pile of shoes by the door as Dad does. Remember that we are always modeling behavior, and our children will eventually mirror it. There is nothing worse than when a parent tells a child to do one thing but does something entirely different. (For example, a father tells a child not to yell at his younger brother but then yells at his wife.) Children learn their behavior from us.

Teach Self-Efficacy

Miss Frizzle, from the nineties PBS television show and the book series *The Magic School Bus*, helped her students develop belief in their own abilities as learners. They went on exciting field trips, discovering locations, creatures, and time periods. She encouraged them to explore, saying, "Take chances, make mistakes, get messy!" She inspired them to develop their self-efficacy.

Like Miss Frizzle, we want to help our children who have ADHD to cope with adversity and to work through difficult challenges. Self-efficacy is the ability to define a target, persevere through challenges, and see oneself as capable. To be clear, I am not talking about self-esteem. Although boosting self-esteem seems essential, helping our children simply feel good about themselves doesn't necessarily help them develop important skills. The best way to help children with ADHD feel good about themselves is to provide them with opportunities to learn what their strengths and skills are. Children who develop self-efficacy learn to believe they can rely on their abilities when facing a challenge. We can help them learn to navigate their lives better when we create opportunities for self-efficacy.

Gently Challenge Negative Thoughts

If your child laments while doing homework, "I'm just stupid!" don't rush to object, because they will most likely dig deeper into their belief. Instead, show empathy and say, "I am so sorry you feel that way. You're frustrated. Do you want to take a break?" After the break, when your child is calm, you can challenge the notion by asking, "What else can we do instead of calling ourselves stupid?" You can teach your child to identify and challenge negative thoughts that undermine their belief in their ability to master a task. Then replace the negative thinking with a positive, truthful idea.

Teach Breaking a Task Down into Small Bits

Teaching children how to break down a job into small, actionable steps helps them learn how to do things. From there, they can develop strategies for persisting in completing those steps when they encounter obstacles. Notice, analyze, and celebrate successes.

You can increase self-efficacy by teaching your children to identify successes and to accurately assess their contribution. Use process praise, such as, "I see that you are making great progress! Tell me what you've done so far." Asking your child to talk about their process and progress will help them learn how to plan future assignments.

Provide Opportunities for Mastery Experiences

Give children opportunities to control their environment, make decisions, use and practice their skills, and try different paths to achieve their goals. For example, for a very young child, you could ask, "Which shoes do you want to wear to church?" For older children, you can use questions such as, "Where do you think is the best place for you to finish your homework? Why is that? How do you know?"

Emphasize Effort

After studying the behavior of thousands of children, Dr. Carol Dweck coined the terms *fixed mindset* and *growth mindset* to describe the underlying beliefs people have about learning and intelligence.[1] When students believe they can get smarter, they understand that effort makes them stronger. Then they put in extra time and effort, and that leads to higher achievement. You can help your children develop their growth mindset by acknowledging and rewarding the amount of effort a task took.

Be Honest and Realistic

When a child fails or has a setback, don't pretend it didn't happen. It is far better to acknowledge the struggle and identify specific strengths the child might use next time. Explain that problem solvers learn from mistakes and move on.

When children develop an understanding that they are capable and that they have skills, they manage their ADHD symptoms differently. Instead of being victims of their disorganized brains, they realize that they have the power to adopt strategies to compensate. They learn that their strategies aren't foolproof, so they keep adapting them.

Developing Resilience

My daughter Kaitlynn loved soccer, and she was a good player. Though school was challenging for her because of her ADHD, she found her place in sports. She played on several teams, developing her talents for the day when she would play varsity for her school. Coaches loved her willingness to learn and work hard on the field. "She takes feedback so quickly," one coach said to me after a game. Kaitlynn had developed a strong sense of self-efficacy on the field. She knew that she could rely on her strengths.

In the spring of her junior year, she tried out for her high school's varsity team. She left the first day of tryouts feeling uneasy. By the third day, she suspected that she wasn't going to make it. "The coach is going to pull up two freshmen. I just know it." She explained how these two young players would most likely play for Division I colleges in the future. They already had recruiters approaching them. The competition for this varsity team was steeper than it had ever been.

The next day, the list was published. Kaitlynn's name wasn't on it.

Crushed by not achieving the goal she'd had for years, she went to the coach and asked what she could do to make the next year's team. "Work on your touches," he said and gave her some other skills to work on too.

Each Sunday afternoon for a full year, Kaitlynn went to the local fieldhouse and practiced the skills the coach mentioned. She continued to work with a private coach and play for travel teams. She was disciplined and focused on her goal of playing varsity. When tryouts came around again, Kaitlynn knew she had trained well.

The team list was posted. Kaitlynn's name wasn't on it. Again.

She had been cut from the team a second time. It didn't make sense. This wasn't how it was supposed to go. "If you put in the effort," she had been told, "you'll achieve your goals." She had no explanation and was devastated. My usually stoic child was broken. For a week, I could hear sobbing coming from her room when I walked by.

I decided to call the coach. His voice was tense. I think he was used to parents screaming at him. I assured him that I wasn't angry with him but needed help. My voice was choked as I asked, "Can you help me explain this to my daughter?"

"Kaitlynn could easily be a starter for any of the teams that we play in our division. She is an excellent player," he said carefully. "But for the past two years, we have had an increase in talent. I've had to cut otherwise outstanding players."

Self-efficacy wasn't enough. Now my child needed to develop resilience.

Resilience is the process of adapting well in the face of adversity, trauma, tragedy, threats, or significant sources of stress. We know that we need to dig into the resilience barrel when one or more of our sources of confidence are affected: self, others, or environment. In Kaitlynn's case, her setback hit her in all three. She was overwhelmingly angry at herself for failing. And not making the team meant that her relationships with others were threatened. She felt like she had lost her group of friends because they would be busy at practice now. School, her environment, would feel very different too. Her senior year felt like a disaster.

Although I knew the research on the importance of developing resilience, it was heartbreaking to watch her struggle. To be entirely honest, and contrary to what I know to be good parenting, if I could have taken away her pain at that moment, I would have. Like most parents, I hate watching the children I dearly love in pain. I couldn't change her situation; I could only provide support.

Kaitlynn would learn that she would recover from this. She discovered that she wasn't alone: she still had familial and social support. And though it would be a while before she could find meaning in what had happened, in a few weeks, Kaitlynn showed signs of purposefully choosing positive emotions and deciding to focus on other hobbies. Though it was a painful experience, she came to see it as a time that forced her personal growth.

I called Kaitlynn and asked if I could include her story in this chapter. She is now twenty-seven, married, and a chiropractor. "Of course," she said. "Make sure you add that if I hadn't been cut for soccer, I wouldn't have developed my basketball skills." She is a baller. She and her six-foot-seven-inch husband still play in basketball tournaments on the weekends. Her sense of resilience turned into a reservoir of strength and served her well in college and graduate school.

For so many children with ADHD, their sense of confidence is reduced each day. They are frequently reminded that they are misfit toys. Their confidence is like a rock that is continually being chipped away as the negative feedback weighs massively more than the positive. Teaching children about resiliency can help them bounce back from everyday stress and challenges. When they are resilient, they are braver, more curious, more adaptable, and more able to extend their reach into the world.

Holding the Hope

As a mom sat in my parenting workshop, her tears spilled out. "Life is just so hard for this little guy." She was referring to her nine-year-old, who was struggling at school and at home. "He gets so frustrated with himself. He cries and worries that he won't grow up okay."

I remembered my own heart aching from watching my kids flounder and stumble. Like this mom, I often wished that I could take away their struggles.

"Will you do me a favor?" I said, my eyes welling with tears. (I'm a sympathetic crier.) "Tell him that he will be okay. Tell him that you know he will grow up to be a strong, smart person who will do big things. And if he can't believe you now, tell him that you will continue to hold that hope for him until he can hold it for himself." I cupped my hands as if holding something fragile. "Remind him each day that you know he will be okay and you are holding his hope for him."

You are your child's greatest gift in this world—or at least you can be. Choose to be your child's champion. Choose empathy over disappointment, love over anger, self-efficacy over fixing blame, and problem-solving over punishment.

Now What?

Writing Your ADHD Story

My clients have heard plenty of theories from friends and family about why they are the way they are. Many people try to help those with ADHD without fully understanding that it is a brain-based disorder. They don't appreciate that the CDC has determined that ADHD is a serious public health concern because of its high prevalence and chronic nature. They don't know that ADHD is not caused by moral failure, poor parenting, family problems, poor teachers or schools, too much video gaming, or food allergies. Their well-meaning but amateur expositions of why ADHD occurs in individuals can be harmful to someone struggling to manage essential day-to-day tasks.

Because of the negative messages around ADHD, my clients often blame themselves—their personalities or their character—for their struggles. They tell me their stories about being misunderstood and frustrated. Through their work with me, they learn that their brains aren't broken. They write new stories that include hope and endurance.

ADHD Is Real—Even for Adults

"My primary care physician told me that adults don't have ADHD," Ginger said. "It is frustrating that many professionals still don't understand what ADHD is and how it affects adults who have it."

Ginger wisely went for a second opinion, but it didn't bring the answers she was seeking. "The second doctor told me I couldn't have ADHD—I'm too smart, I did well in school, I don't have behavioral problems, and I'm a high-functioning professional. I wanted to cry. The doctor had no idea how hard it was for me to look like I have it all together." Ginger was tired of defending her mental abilities. "I saw how people looked at me when I made an ADHD careless error, like when I put the wrong date on my notes. They rolled their eyes and acted like I'm an absentminded professor or, worse, that I'm incompetent." Although she expressed her frustration with others, she was also disappointed in herself. "I want to scream that making a small mistake doesn't make me stupid, but at the same time, I felt stupid."

Ginger kept reading about ADHD. "I just knew that I had it. I mean, I saw myself in every article about it. It explained so much." She continued her search and eventually found a doctor who specialized in treating ADHD. Although there is no single test to definitively check for ADHD, there are several assessments that can guide a skilled clinician in making an accurate diagnosis. Fortunately for Ginger, she was diagnosed and appropriately medicated. The diagnosis made a huge difference for her. "I was just so relieved that someone understood me."

The medication that she took for ADHD helped her pay attention to the small details of her job. She also went to ADHD coaching to find more strategies to maximize her performance.

"Oh, it's still tricky. I still make mistakes. But now I have more confidence in my ability to anticipate and solve problems." Ginger is continuing to write her ADHD story with strategies like using her past, present, and future self (chapter 6) and the Solve-It Grid (chapter 8) to help her manage her job's menial tasks.

ADHD Doesn't Always Look the Same

As with other disorders, ADHD symptoms are expressed differently in different people. One person's symptoms may be problems with impulsivity and organization. Another person's may be the inability to begin a task or manage their frustration levels. "I don't look like I have ADHD," Kyle said when I asked him what he wanted others to know about his story. "I want people to understand what the symptoms of ADHD really are."

Kyle was twenty-six when he first met me in my office. At that time he told me, "I'm usually the most mellow guy in the group. But people don't realize that my mind is dashing." Kyle's easygoing personality enabled him to blend in and go with the flow. Externally, he looked peaceful and present. But internally, he felt overwhelmed. "I have trouble listening and focusing on what is happening around me because so much is happening." His focus and thoughts bounced around. "Some people still think that those with ADHD have a shortage of attention or are hyper. It's just the opposite." He described how his mental hyperactivity caused him to pay too much attention to everything much of the time.

He's right; many assume that the hyperactivity that accompanies the disorder means physically wiggling around in your seat. In fact, the vast majority of adults with ADHD are not overtly hyperactive, though they are hyperactive internally.[1] Kyle fit that definition.

Medication and coaching helped Kyle manage the chaos he felt in his head. Now he has confidently calmed his internal dialogues and has increased his sense of being present in a situation.

Specifically, he focused on using his divergent thinking patterns strategically (chapter 4) and not letting all of the rabbits loose at once.

Kyle described how his torrent of thoughts led to feelings of inadequacy. He explained that his anxiety and fear of failure used up most of his concentration. "I was stuck in a paradox," he learned after coaching. "My attention is destroyed by the fear of my lack of attention." All of the thoughts swirling in his head took too much of his energy. He learned that he had been using malicious motivation (chapter 6) to get himself to accomplish even the most basic of tasks.

Like so many other individuals, Kyle forgot what was good about himself. "I lost confidence in myself. I was losing hope." He was locked in a tenacious holding pattern of just coping with his life and keeping his head above water. Through coaching, he was able to see that even when he felt like he was drowning, he demonstrated considerable emotional health and was able to climb the ladder (chapter 10).

Kyle's ADHD story is hopeful now. "I learned how to manage my ADHD," he said. ADHD cannot be cured, but many treatment options exist, including parental coaching, school accommodations, ADHD coaching, specialized therapy, and medications. "I don't feel like I'm on the outside looking in anymore!" Kyle said. "Though it's still a lot of work, it's not nearly as difficult as it was before."

So many of my clients are victors. They courageously show up in their daily lives and appear to hold it all together, even when it isn't easy to do so. As you have seen from the stories in this book, ADHD significantly impacts family life, peer relationships, and school performance. The stress of trying to look normal can lead to problems with self-esteem, anxiety, and even feelings of depression.

Now What?

Throughout this book, you've read the stories of many people with ADHD. Now let's take a look at your ADHD story.

Take some time to consider how ADHD has affected your life. What symptoms create the biggest difficulty for you? Where do you want to take your ADHD story? What are your next steps? Let's start with reorienting and recalibrating. I've also included some of these questions in appendix B, with room to fill in your answers.

Reorienting yourself is like looking at a map and figuring out where you are on it. Use this book to reorient yourself. Take a few moments to reflect on what you have thought about while reading, using these prompts:

This book made me understand that . . .

This book made me hope that . . .

This book made me wish that . . .

This book made me decide that . . .

This book made me look at . . .

This book made me believe that . . .

This book made me remember that . . .

This book made me wonder if . . .

This book made me want to . . .

Recalibrating yourself means adjusting your course to make sure you are on the right track. Follow the next steps to adjust the course of your story.

First, review what you've written. Circle three of the sentences about the book that are the most important to you.

Second, consider the following questions:

1. Why are those sentences important to you?

    For example, I wrote, "This book made me understand that my emotions are affecting my entire family. I want to manage my emotions better so that my family life will be better."

2. Was there a chapter that you found particularly useful? Why did it resonate with you?

For example: "I'm going to review chapter 3 about big emotions because I have been losing patience at work lately." Or, "I'm going to reread chapter 6 about the mistaken ways I motivate myself because I think I use some or all of them."

3. What action item can you create out of your important sentences?

To create an action item, answer these basics: What will you do? When will you do it? How will you do it? For example: (1) "I'm going to reread the chapter on the Emotional Health Ladder." (2) "I'm going to use the Emotional Health Ladder each morning, noon, and evening to increase my emotional awareness."

How will you remember this action item? We often create great goals, but we forget to do what we proposed. Create a simple plan to remind yourself of your intention. For example: "I've placed an alert on my calendar for eight o'clock each morning. That is my reminder to look at the ladder and to check in on my self-awareness."

4. Who can help you?

Who have you welcomed into your yard who you can ask to help you? What can they do to help you develop stronger skills? Do you need the outside support of a coach, counselor, or psychiatrist?

Many people effectively managing their ADHD live the lives they have always wanted to. They learn to gather their scattered thoughts and feelings to accomplish what they set out to do. Their skills, strategies, and techniques help them not only survive but thrive.

What about you? Think of the messages you've picked up over the years from others about yourself or ADHD. Are they true?

What do you want people to know about you or your ADHD? How will you communicate that message to them?

Never forget, this is *your* unique ADHD story. You are the main character of this story that will contain challenges and conflicts, setbacks and forward motion, failures and victories. Those are all a part of your story. With the tools and techniques you have learned and will continue learning, you will be able to put ADHD in its rightful place—as one of many characters in the story *you* are writing. How you write the next chapters is up to you.

Appendix A

Your Life on the Grid

Use the following to clarify your understanding of quadrants.

Tasks that are usually in the Yellow Quadrant:

_____

What is it about these tasks that make them Yellow for you?

_____

Tasks that are usually in the Red Quadrant:

_____

What is it about these tasks that make them Red for you?

_____

Tasks that are usually in the Blue Quadrant:

_____

What is it about these tasks that make them Blue for you?

_____

Tasks that are usually in the Green Quadrant:

_____

What is it about these tasks that make them Green for you?

_____

Use the following questions to help you tackle Yellow tasks.

Before you begin:

1. What task do you want to accomplish? _____

   _____

2. What makes this a Yellow task for you? _____

   _____

3. Why does it need to be done? _____

   _____

4. When do you want to begin the task? (Block out the time on your calendar.) _____

   _____

5. Plan how you will accomplish this task. (Be specific. Write a how-to list of the steps you need to take in order.) ____

   _____

6. Look at your how-to list and plan how you will actually begin. (Where will you work? What will you need around you?) _____

   _____

7. How will you handle distractions and get back on track? What might be emotionally distracting to you while you work? How will you manage that? How will you guard yourself against malicious motivators? _____

_____

8. How will you know when you are finished? (This step helps you avoid the perfection trap.) _____

_____

9. Set a timer for twenty minutes or less and begin.

When the timer alerts you:

1. Take a deep breath. How are you doing? (If you have hit a great rhythm with your task, make a note of your progress and keep going! If not, go to the next step.) _____

_____

2. What is blocking you from completing this task? _____

_____

   a. Is it an emotional reason (e.g., you just hate this work so much that you don't want to do it)? If so, take a break and go to a timed Blue Quadrant activity. Attempt the task again after the break.
   b. Is it a technical reason (e.g., you don't have the information you need)? If so, take a break and go to a timed Blue Quadrant activity. Write down what you need in order to complete the task. Rewrite your how-to list. Set the timer.
   c. Is it a cognitive reason (e.g., you don't understand how to complete this)? If so, take a break and go to a timed Blue Quadrant activity. Write down what you don't understand or know. How will you learn what you

need? What resources could you use to fill in this gap? Rewrite your how-to list. Set the timer.

When you finish the Yellow task:

1. Congratulate yourself. You did it! You conquered a task that you were tempted to avoid or procrastinate about.
2. What went well for you? What did you do that helped you complete this task? _____

   _____

3. How can you remember to use this strategy with your next Yellow task? _____

   _____

Appendix B

Writing Your ADHD Story

Use these questions to take a look at your ADHD story.

1. How has ADHD affected your life? What symptoms create the biggest difficulty for you? _____
   _____

2. Think of the messages you've picked up over the years from others about yourself or ADHD. Are they true? What do you want people to know about you or your ADHD? How will you communicate that message to them?_____
   _____

3. Where do you want to take your ADHD story? What do you want to do? _____
   _____

4. Reorient yourself by taking a few moments to reflect on what you have thought about while reading this book, using these prompts:
   This book made me understand that _____
   _____

This book made me hope that _____

_____

This book made me wish that _____

_____

This book made me decide that _____

_____

This book made me look at _____

_____

This book made me believe that _____

_____

This book made me remember that _____

_____

This book made me wonder if _____

_____

This book made me want to _____

_____

5. Recalibrate yourself by reviewing what you've written. Circle three of the sentences about the book that are the most important to you. Why are they important? _____

_____

6. What chapter of this book could help you address the sentences you wrote? _____

7. What action item can you create out of your important sentences?

    a. Action: _____

    _____

    b. How/when I will implement it: _____

    _____

8. Who can help you? What can they do to help you develop stronger skills? Do you need the outside support of a coach, counselor, or psychiatrist? _____

_____

Appendix C

If You Love Someone Who Has ADHD

Perhaps you don't have ADHD, but you've picked up this book because you are in a relationship with someone who does. Parts of this book might have been confusing for you. For example, it can be difficult to understand how loud noises, clutter, paying bills, and household chores can send your partner over the edge. You may still secretly wonder, even after reading this book, if they are really trying hard enough.

You love their brilliant, buzzing mind, but you find yourself exhausted by them. You know that your loved one is capable of tremendous things—with a little support and positive reinforcement. But you have feelings too. You may feel lonely, ignored, unappreciated, and like you are the only grown-up in the house. You don't feel like you can rely on your partner. You're tired of taking care of everything on your own and being the only responsible party in the relationship.

It is important to learn how to manage your own emotions and expectations. You can learn how to react to frustrations in ways that encourage and motivate your partner. Consider the following as you develop a plan with them.

Separate who your partner is from their symptoms or behaviors. What ADHD symptom bothers you the most? Why does it bother you so much? What feeling does it evoke in you? How can you reframe it so that you don't take it personally? How will you remember that your partner's symptoms aren't character traits?

Improve communication. How can you be honest about how you are feeling without being critical of your partner? How can you guard yourself from making assumptions about your partner's motivations? (For example: "If he loved me, he'd remember to take the trash out.")

Find the humor in the situation. How can you bring levity back to your relationship, especially over the inevitable miscommunications and misunderstandings?

Increase teamwork. How can the two of you build on each other's strengths? What can you do to rebalance the workload around the house? How can you clearly define and divide tasks? How will you get outside help if you are both weak in a certain area? (For example, if neither of you is good with money, you could hire a bookkeeper or research money-management apps that make budgeting easier.)

Having ADHD has a serious effect on one's life and the lives of those who love them. You and your loved ones can build understanding, learn effective strategies, and develop new skills as you accommodate for their ADHD symptoms.

Appendix D

Resources for Those
with ADHD

ADDitude magazine: additudemag.com.

The American Professional Society of ADHD and Related Disorders (APSARD): apsard.org. This society provides research on ADHD throughout its life span, as well as evidence-based practices and education.

Attention Deficit Disorder Association (ADDA): add.org.

Children and Adults with Attention-Deficit/Hyperactivity Disorder (CHADD): chadd.org. This is a nonprofit organization serving individuals with ADHD and their families.

International conference on ADHD: chadd.org. Participants include adults with ADHD, parents and caregivers of children with ADHD, educators, mental health clinicians, coaches, advocates, and medical professionals who diagnose and treat patients with ADHD.

Appendix E

What Is ADHD Coaching?

ADHD coaches encourage individuals with ADHD to stay focused on their goals, develop resilience when they face obstacles, and feel better about the way they engage with their lives. They are specifically trained and certified to help their clients manage their lives more effectively.

Research shows that ADHD coaching can improve symptoms, executive functioning related behaviors, self-esteem, well-being, and quality of life. Coaches who specialize in working with clients who have ADHD will often educate their clients about ADHD and how it affects them across a lifetime. Building on that awareness, coaches support their clients in creating systems and strategies that help them manage the practical aspects of life.

To find a coach, visit the ADHD Coaches Organization at www .adhdcoaches.org/find-your-coach. Many ADHD coaches work virtually, on Zoom, Skype, or other platforms. The price of coaching varies depending on where you live and who you hire. While ADHD coaching is not covered by insurance, some experts may offer a sliding-scale payment plan.

NOTES

Chapter 1 And Then *Ping!* Goes My Brain

1. William Dodson, "Secrets of Your ADHD Brain," *ADDitude*, November 9, 2020, https://www.additudemag.com/secrets-of-the-adhd-brain/.

Chapter 4 Following the Rabbit

1. Lewis Carroll, *Alice's Adventures in Wonderland* (Chicago: Volume One Publishing, 1998), 3.
2. *Gilmore Girls*, season 7, episode 11, "Santa's Secret Stuff," directed by Lee Shallat Chemel, written by Amy Sherman-Palladino and Rebecca Kirshner, aired January 23, 2007.
3. *Gilmore Girls*, season 7, episode 11.
4. Carroll, *Alice's Adventures in Wonderland*, 191–92.

Chapter 5 The Monsters We Face

1. Michel de Montaigne, *The Complete Essays of Montaigne*, trans. Donald M. Frame (Stanford, CA: Stanford University Press, 1976).

Chapter 6 Malicious Motivation

1. Russell A. Barkley, *ADHD and the Nature of Self-Control* (New York: Guilford, 2005).
2. J. E. LeDoux, *The Emotional Brain: The Mysterious Underpinnings of Emotional Life* (New York: Simon & Schuster, 1996).
3. The concept of malicious motivators was first published in ADDitude, www.additudemag.com/how-to-motivate-adhd-brain-emotional-health/.
4. Brené Brown, *Daring Greatly: How the Courage to Be Vulnerable Transforms the Way We Live, Love, Parent, and Lead* (New York: Gotham Books, 2012), 69.

Chapter 7 Solving Motivational Murders

1. *Dr. Who*, season 3, episode 10, "Blink," directed by Hettie Macdonald, written by Steven Moffat, aired June 9, 2007.
2. For two studies on ADHD and time perception, see Radek Ptacek et al., "Clinical Implications of the Perception of Time in Attention Deficit Hyperactivity Disorder (ADHD): A Review," *Medical Science Monitor* 25 (2019): 3918–24, doi.org/10.12659/MSM.914225; and Hom-Yi Lee and En-Lin Yang, "Exploring the Effects of Working Memory on Time Perception in Attention Deficit Hyperactivity Disorder," *Psychological Reports* 122 (2019): 23–35, doi:10.1177/0033 294118755674.
3. Emi Furukawa et al., "Abnormal Striatal BOLD Responses to Reward Anticipation and Reward Delivery in ADHD," *PLoS ONE* 9, no. 2 (February 2014), doi:10.1371/journal.pone.0089129.

Chapter 8 Living on the Grid

1. The concept of the Solve-It Grid was first published in *ADDitude*, www .additudemag.com/time-on-your-side/.

Chapter 10 Climbing the Ladder

1. Thomas E. Brown, "Exaggerated Emotions: How and Why ADHD Triggers Intense Feelings," *ADDitude*, accessed February 15, 2021, www.additudemag.com /slideshows/adhd-emotions-understanding-intense-feelings/.

Chapter 11 Welcome Home

1. See Revelation 3:20.

Chapter 12 Dancing through the Day

1. Rachel Fargason, Brittney White, and Karen Gamble, "Complete Sleep-Wake Cycle Reversal Related to ADHD Detected by Actigraphy," *Annals of Clinical Psychiatry* 25 (2013): E8–E9.
2. Shawn Stevenson, *Sleep Smarter: 21 Essential Strategies to Sleep Your Way to a Better Body, Better Health, and Bigger Success* (New York: Rodale Books, 2012).
3. Stevenson, *Sleep Smarter*.
4. Stevenson, *Sleep Smarter*.

Chapter 13 The Island of Misfit Toys

1. Carol Dweck, *Mindset: The New Psychology of Success* (New York: Random House, 2006).

Chapter 14 Now What?

1. Dodson, "Secrets of Your ADHD Brain."

Tamara Rosier, PhD, is founder of the ADHD Center of West Michigan, where she and her staff work with individuals with ADHD and their families to help them learn strategies and develop new skills to live effectively with ADHD. Dr. Rosier is also the president of the ADHD Coaches Organization. She is a popular conference and keynote speaker, is a frequent guest on podcasts, and has published numerous articles about living with ADHD. She lives in West Michigan.